Now We're Talking

Creating Connection through Authentic Conversations with Your Teenage Daughter

By

MIRIAM ARVINGER

Miriam Arvinger. ©2022

All rights reserved. No part of this book may be reproduced, stored, or transmitted by any means- whether auditory, graphic, mechanical, or electronic- without written permission of both publisher and author, except in the case of brief excerpts used in critical articles and certain other noncommercial uses permitted by copyright law. Unauthorized reproduction of any part of this work is illegal and is punishable by law.

ISBN: 979-8-9872605-0-0 (Paperback)

eISBN: 979-8-9872605-1-7 (eBook)

Library of Congress Control Number: 2022922322

Because of the dynamic nature of the internet, any web addresses or links contained in this book may have changed since publication and may no longer be valid.

Printed in the United States of America
Cover Design: Ayoola Cheakina (www.fiverr.com/cheakina)
Photo: Ashley Crawley of Still Shots Photography
Editors: Cindy Draughon (www.fiverr.com/cldraughon)
      The Writing Expert

      Visit www.miriamarvinger.com
   for additional information and resources.

Dedication

WOW!...This is really happening. Books have been in my soul for over 25 years. I have always wanted to write and I get ideas for books almost daily. I have had so many ideas that I would start, and start, and start and never finish. As a matter of fact, I have written about 10 starts! The more I think about writing, the more ideas I discover. So finishing this book is epic for me and I have many people to thank:

I will begin with my one and only Savior, King, Lord and Friend, Jesus, the Christ - without Him, there is no me. This is part of His will and purpose for me and I am tremendously blessed by Him daily. Thank you God so very much for being everything I need.

Thank you to my children Tiara and Corey - you teach me more than you know and make me better everyday. One woman shouldn't have this much wealth.

Thank you to my mom and dad (RIP) - my support system. You weren't perfect, but you did your very best and made me believe I could do anything.

Thank you to my sister, Jackie (RIP) and my niece and nephew Shanta and Quincy - Family over everything. You always make me smile, feel needed and loved.

Thank you to Latrayer, Deaner and Bronwyn - My sistas and aces. 40+ years of amazing friendship, laughter and love. I feel like I can conquer the world with you all by my side.

Thank you to my book coaches Jasmine Womack and Tonya Carter - Your spirit of excellence and thorough, no-nonsense coaching allowed me to finally realize my dream of becoming a best-selling author. I am grateful.

Finally, to every young girl, some now women with their own daughters, who allowed me into some part of your lives as a teacher, coach, minister, auntie, mentor, big sister or friend, I thank you for trusting me with those fragile parts of your lives. Thank you for teaching me how to listen, understand, serve and love better. I truly love you.

It's hard to explain what each of you mean to me, but I pray that my love for you is seen and felt. Thank you all for loving me so well.

Table of Contents

Dedication _____ iii

Introduction _____ vi

Chapter One: You Were Made For This _____ 1

Chapter Two: What's Really Going On? _____ 11

Chapter Three: What's Your Story? _____ 21

Chapter Four: Unlearning _____ 37

Chapter Five: Mindset Matters _____ 53

Chapter Six: Seek To Understand _____ 65

Chapter Seven: Be Proactive _____ 81

Chapter Eight: Unlocking Your Communication Blocks _____ 93

Chapter Nine: You Have The Power _____ 109

Epilogue _____ 119

Meet The Author _____ 126

Appendix _____ 128

Resources For Further Help _____ 128

Introduction

Thank you for picking up this book. I invite you on an amazing but challenging journey to better understand, communicate, and connect with your teenage daughter. I know you may think she's turned into an alien. Your hugs and kisses are no longer welcomed. Her hearing is now impaired, and her vocabulary has dwindled down to a few sarcastic words.

BUT there is hope. The hope that you will build a connection with your daughter that encourages authentic communication and understanding. With this connection she will have what you did not - a safe space to talk about the celebrations and woes of teenagehood and life. And because you created and welcomed this space, your daughter can become strong, confident and bold in her decisions and her journey into womanhood.

Raising teenagers is hard. Raising well-rounded, informed, confident teenage girls can be hell. But it doesn't have to be. If they would only listen and take our good, sound advice all would be well, right? How did that work for you? It didn't. Because 90 percent of the women I interviewed for this book confirmed that open, honest communication with the person they wanted to understand them most, their mothers, wasn't available at all, or in the capacity they wanted. We couldn't talk openly with our mothers about sex, dating, our bodies, boys, girls, etc. and I want to change that. I want to help you foster those meaningful conversations that were hard for your mom to have, and even maybe hard for you to have, so you can be fully connected and included in your daughter's life.

You might say at this point, "I don't know how to begin these conversations." And you probably remember that your mother didn't model this type of interaction with you, most likely because she wasn't comfortable talking about personal things like your period, body issues or dating. You might even say, "Besides, my daughter doesn't want to talk to me. When I approach her about these topics, she just ignores me or puts talking off. When I try to talk to her about teenage life, it's just awkward. I was told that children should just do as they're told."

Do any of these words sound familiar? If so, I hear you, and as Mrs. Doubtfire would say, "Help is on the way!" (I loved Mrs. Doubtfire by the way. She had balls…literally :)

This book is not a one stop fix all. Parenting a daughter is a skill set in itself, and it takes time to develop the communication and mindset skills needed to make the connection with your preteen or teenage daughter. But I have confidence in you and know you can do it. My intention is to offer insight into what I have gleaned from working with thousands of girls and women over the span of my 35 years of teaching, mentoring and coaching. Hard to believe? Allow me to summarize for you.

I am a mother of one fantastic adult daughter. I've taught middle school for 32 years, been in youth ministry for 27 years, created and implemented an award-winning mentorship program for high school girls for four years, ran an afterschool program for three years, coached cheerleading in two states for 17 years, was a Big Sister for three years, volunteered with Girl Scouts for three years and have been mentoring since I was 20. Whew! I got tired just writing that. So, doing the rough math, I've had the opportunity to interact with thousands of girls from kindergarten age to adult. That's a lot of estrogen! All of those experiences contributed to my knowledge about the wonderful species we call female.

Countless girls have shared with me things they want to know about sensitive topics, growing up and just being a girl. I have answered many questions ranging from, "How many holes do I have down there?" to "What does puberty mean?" I've explained everything from what happens when you get your period to why you have odor under your arms. These young ladies wished they could have asked their mothers but didn't feel comfortable doing so. Fortunately, they had an auntie big sister mentor (ABSM) - me! I literally LOVE talking about this stuff, and I have built that know, like and trust factor with them, and they believe I genuinely care about them, which I do.

You see, working with youth - especially girls, is my gift and calling. I find great joy and satisfaction in it, and I am happiest when I can make a young girl feel good about herself and understand the wonderful being the Creator made her to be. I have never been afraid to talk about these hard topics and I am going to share with you how I do it. Of course, these were not my own daughters so it was easier to talk to them about sensitive things. It can be more challenging when talking to your own daughter. And I realize that, so this book will help you bridge that gap by providing insight into what your daughter wants from you.

Now rarely does someone come to you with information like this that they've gleaned from thousands of girls. Most people who write books like this are coming from the experience of either their own personal relationships with their daughters, or a psychological or therapeutic relationship with girls. My unique positioning is that I am coming to you from what I like to call an ABSM approach - auntie, big sister and mentor. You know, the people we actually did talk to about sensitive topics. The aunt you talked to about the boy you liked. Or the big sister who you talked to about why your breasts were sensitive. Or the mentor from church or your afterschool program that helped you understand positive ways to handle your emotions instead of cutting.

I wanted to be the voice of the girls I have worked with over the years. I always encourage them to talk to their mothers. Some have tried and some just won't. We will look at the reasons why. I hope to help you be the one or at least one of the ones that your daughter goes to with her concerns.

As a mom, I would love to tell you that I had it all figured out when it came to raising my daughter to be healthy, happy, and whole, but I did not. I made so many mistakes. The truth is, I was a single parent of two children (a son and a daughter). Raising my children was tough, especially raising my daughter. Mainly because girls tend to be more private, more emotional and less open to discussing what they are actually going through. This can lead to speculation and disconnection.

Did you dream of the type of relationship with your daughter where you laughed at each other's jokes, wore matching outfits, bonded over deep conversations and hung out together by choice? Yeah, me too. While me and my daughter's relationship wasn't horrible, I know some of the barriers I put up and my lack of self-awareness contributed to unnecessary struggles in her life and mine. I had an advantage, though. I worked with girls for most of my life. So, what I gleaned from their experiences and stories helped me navigate the issues I faced with my daughter. I heard directly from the girls' mouths what they wanted from their moms but didn't get. I also got to observe what mothers did that closed off communication and connection. The things I learned are what is shared in this book.

To improve communication with my daughter I had to become more self-aware of my past, my triggers, and my trauma, and understand how those things were affecting our ability to talk and share. I had to understand all the nuances my daughter's generation faced, things I did not have to deal with when I was growing up. I had to learn to build a connection with my daughter even though I didn't have one with my own mother. Many of us are trying to mother our daughters in a season we weren't mothered. I had to learn to be vulnerable and authentic with my daughter if

I wanted her to show up the same way. And while no relationship is perfect, I had to become who I needed to be to foster a better relationship with my daughter, and as she matured and I grew in understanding, our relationship continued to evolve organically.

Has it been challenging? Yes. Being open and vulnerable about your story and the ugly parts of your life ain't easy. There are things you just don't want your children to know. There are things you want to forget. There are things you are embarrassed about. You don't need to tell your daughter everything, but you do have to confront your stuff. Because unhealed stuff will rear its ugly head every time. In working with girls, I had to be vulnerable, authentic and understanding. It is the secret sauce to connecting with them, and the rewards are worth it.

I would say I am blessed to be able to help girls the way I have. I count it a privilege to be there for them and to listen as they share their struggles with me. I love seeing my former mentees and students today in their adult lives. So many have not repeated the patterns of their past. Many have gained self-confidence and knowledge about who they are. They are grateful to have had a voice and are providing the same for their own daughters. We still reminisce about our times together and how they thought being a pre-teen or teen was the end of the world. I am grateful to have played some part in their lives that empowered them to form better relationships, and that's exactly what I would want to help you do.

Each of the book's chapters will begin with a letter to mothers from real girls or women whom I've had the pleasure of mentoring over the years. The letters are either going to talk about how they would have liked to communicate with their mothers or how they did communicate with their mothers, and then I will take it from there. Most of the names have been changed to protect their privacy.

Reading this book alone won't help you. You have to do something and at the end of each chapter, I will have a question, an action and an affirmation. Please answer the questions honestly. They are designed to help you become more self-aware and identify your communication blocks. Then you will have an action step. Something I want you to DO. Again, reading alone is not enough. Action is required. The last thing in each chapter is an affirmation. And that's just a word of encouragement that I want you to repeat every day so that you can gain the confidence and skills you need to communicate effectively with your daughter. So, if you're ready for this journey, I'm right here by your side willing to help. Let's do it!

Believing in you,
Miriam

Chapter One

YOU WERE MADE FOR THIS

Dear Mom,

I wish I would have been able to talk to you about the things that were bothering me when I was a teenager. For example, things like why my breasts were small and my butt was big and how boys used to look at me and I felt awkward. What happens when I get my period? And I would have loved to learn about good touches and bad touches, because I had a few of those bad touches and was afraid to tell you. I thought you wouldn't believe me or think I was responsible.

I know you had a lot on you because you were a single mom of 5, but those are the things that I wish I could have come to you about. I was afraid. Instead, I looked for advice from my friends, and sometimes learned from my older sisters and some of my after-school counselors. I hoped that you would give me the answers to some things about my body so I would not have felt so insecure, or like I was different. I know it was hard for you to do so because you were taught to be seen and not heard and you had your own insecurities. I know no one talked to you about your body and all the questions you had about sex, dating, boys, etc. and I know your childhood was traumatic. I know your mother didn't allow you the opportunity to speak about those things and she definitely didn't answer any of your questions because she didn't raise you. However, I sometimes wish that you would have done something a little differently than what you experienced or got the help you needed to be comfortable in your own skin. At any rate, eventually I did find answers, but those are some of the things that I wish I could have talked to you about. I know it would have made us closer and saved me some heartache and pain. I suppose you did the best you could with what you knew.

I love you,
Miriam, 58

This letter could have probably been written by many daughters. Daughters who would have loved the opportunity to talk to their mothers about things that were important to them. I also know that most mothers would also have loved the opportunity to talk to their daughters about things that their mothers may have neglected to share with them, but just didn't know how or have the tools to do so. Do you see how the lack of communication and knowledge can be generational?

This is why it is so important to apply what I teach you in this book. You can begin to change the narrative of your daughter's generation. She can then apply what she's learned and help her daughter, and so on. You are either building bridges or burning them. You build bridges by finding out what you need to know and applying it. You burn bridges by doing the same thing that isn't working but expecting different results.

YOU GOT THIS

I want you to get excited and motivated as you begin this journey, no matter where you are starting from. You may have a younger daughter about to enter her pre-teens. This is an amazing position to be in because she is not quite in the stage of completely shutting you out and keeping secrets. You may have a daughter smack dab in the middle of adolescence. Here's where you'll get plenty of opportunities to practice new skills. Or you may have a daughter in her late teens or even an adult daughter that you still have trouble communicating and connecting with and you want to change that. Whatever stage of life your daughter is in, you can use what I share and what you already know about being a girl to help create connection. I don't want you to feel like it's too early or it's too late. The time to do something new is as soon as you learn that there is something new that you can do to reach your desired goal. I want to be your biggest cheerleader on this journey, so I will often say: YOU GOT THIS!

YOU WERE A TEENAGER ONCE

The fact that you are a mother and you knew exactly what it felt like as a teenage girl to not have that connection with your mother, makes you more than capable of creating new practices. Being mindful of those memories and feelings will help you understand what your daughter may be experiencing. Many times, mothers don't tap into their teenage selves when raising daughters. I realize that the teenage years may have been traumatic, confusing and unpleasant. But it's those very feelings and emotions that should encourage change.

Do you remember when you said: If I have a daughter, I am going to make sure she…well, now we're here. You know exactly what you needed and wanted from your mother as a teenage girl. You wanted to be seen and heard. You wanted the freedom to express yourself without fear, condemnation or judgment. You wanted to feel safe expressing yourself and asking questions. You wanted to be vulnerable about what was going on in your mind and body. But for whatever reasons, you couldn't. So the mere fact that you have walked this walk before equips you for this journey. I also realize that you can't give what you don't have. So having the tools I provide will give you what you need to communicate better with your daughter.

YOU CAN DO HARD THINGS

Have you ever wanted to quit being a mother? I see your hand. Transparent moment: I have. As a single mother, with 2 small children only one year apart, life was very challenging. I was taking care of 2 babies and working full time as a teacher. I had just ended a relationship and moved to a new state where I knew very few people and had little support. Because of my income, I didn't live in the best neighborhood. Home was stressful, work was stressful and taking care of my babies was stressful. They needed love and constant attention, and I was on empty most days.

I remember coming home from work one evening with one baby in my arms and one holding my hand. I had stopped by the grocery store on my way home, so I had grocery bags hanging from my arms as well. As I approached my apartment, I noticed a young man standing under the stairs smoking. I became nervous, because something in me told me to hurry up. I began walking up the stairs to my apartment, practically dragging my daughter. When I got to the top of the stairs, I noticed him coming around the corner to come up the stairs. I promise you, something in me (my God) said, pretend like someone is in the house and start yelling at them. I quickly opened the door (by that time he was almost at the top of the stairs) and started yelling, "Mark, come help me with these kids, you see me struggling. Didn't you hear me knocking?" As I was entering my apartment, I saw him pause at the top of the stairs before walking slowly toward me. I hurried in and locked the door and continued to have a loud argument with

"Mark" about why he was just laying around and not helping me. Listen, I even deepened my voice to pretend like there were 2 people in the apartment, although it was just me and the kids. I was terrified and believed that God spared me from something terrible. That night I put a chair up to the doorknob and slept in the bathtub with my babies. I also cried, because motherhood was hard. Raising my children alone and in these conditions was not what I had planned for my life and I wanted to quit. Of course, I didn't, but I wanted to quit and start again.

Through my faith in God, my family and a move to North Carolina, I got it together. But it was hard - hard to keep the bills paid, find reliable sitters, raise my children with morals and values, provide for their emotional needs, etc. But each day I looked at them, I received new faith that I could do hard things. You know why? Because they were depending on me, and I refused to let them down.

What about you mom? Your daughter is depending on you to guide her and show her how to be a bold, confident woman and how to navigate life's challenges and detours. She is wanting you to understand and connect with her, even though sometimes it may be hard to do so. Will you look at her and tell her that you can do hard things and so can she?

Motherhood is hard, but you can do hard things. I believe you have done plenty of hard things already - finishing school, giving birth, excelling in your career, writing a book, managing a household, driving in Atlanta (lol) - whatever it is, you already have proof that you can do hard things and this is no different. I hope to help make your connection with your daughter a bit easier. You are doing the hardest job you'll ever love, and you're doing it so well. How do I know? You picked up this book to improve your communication and connection with your daughter so you can build a better relationship and break generational strongholds of insecurity and fear. Anyone who seeks help in an area where they want to improve, I consider them a rock star. So you go mama!

IMPOSTER SYNDROME BE GONE

I know you may be feeling a bit of imposter syndrome. You know the feeling that, hey, I'm not built for this. I don't have the right words to say. I don't have the correct tools. My mother didn't talk to me about these things, so how can I talk to my daughter about these things? And yes, many adult women still carry around misinformation and biases around sexuality, identity and self worth.

I understand and know the imposter syndrome all too well. Even in writing this book, I have experienced it. I hoped I would have known about the things I am about to share with you before I raised my daughter and made so many mistakes. I wish I could tell you that I had it all together. I wish I could tell you that my daughter and I have the relationship of my dreams - we hang out, laugh, talk, share secrets, she tells me all about her romantic interests, hopes, desires AND listens intently to all my advice without rolling her eyes or disagreeing with any of it. But that's not my story and that's ok. Throughout my children's lives, I've made plenty of mistakes, but I forgave myself and moved on. And I want you to do the same. Living in the past prevents progress. Giving yourself grace and forgiveness is necessary for success on this journey. We all need it and God gave it to us, so let's receive it.

PROGRESS OVER PERFECTION

Over the years, my daughter and my relationship has made tremendous progress in communication and trust, mainly due to the changes I made within me. Not because I had all the answers. I realized that I needed to adjust my communication style and unproductive habits because what I was doing wasn't working. I needed to provide an environment where she felt safe and comfortable. As an adult, I needed to take the lead and show her how to build trust and to communicate effectively. I had to be willing to change, grow and learn what I didn't know. That's exactly what you are doing now - learning and growing. I also had to remember that it would take time. It's a process and I would make progress as I implemented new strategies, but I didn't have to be perfect and neither do you.

CHAPTER CONCLUSION

You can have a great, mutually respectful relationship with your pre-teen/teenage daughter even though sometimes she feels like a stranger. Society will tell you that teenagers are disrespectful, rude and buck authority. I refuse to listen to that because that is not my story. I know hundreds of wonderful, respectful, smart, compassionate teenagers. You have the answers within you. You know you and what you need to work on, and you know your daughter and what she responds best to. And you have this book. That's half the battle.

You are fearfully and wonderfully made by the Creator. God gave you a womb and you were literally built to carry a child thus be a mother. **MAJOR KEY: You have motherhood in your DNA, so while there is no manual for motherhood, there is an innate calling and ability for you to mother, nurture, create, guide and lead.** You were built for this, so I know you can do it. You are an awesome mother. (Yup, I'm going to pump you up and toot your horn throughout this book.) Toot! Toot!

Remember, it's okay to ask for help. I have asked for help many times when I was stuck with what to say to my own daughter. Asking for help is a sign of strength, not weakness. You will make progress day by day, but please don't seek perfection. It takes time to build new relational habits.

You are here because you want to do better. You want to improve communication and connection with your daughter. You want to increase your bond with her so she can be healthy, whole and know who she is. That's what we all want for our children. I see so many women and I'm sure you do too, who are still suffering from some of the things they had to learn on their own or because they didn't have correct information. I see so many women suffering from identity issues and self-esteem issues because they don't know who they are because they did not have these conversations with their mothers or other trusted adults. I see so many women who struggle in relationships because they didn't have the tools or the guidance that they needed to foster healthy relationships. I see so many women who don't understand womanhood and femininity. We can change that together.

QUESTIONS

What is your goal in reading this book? What stood out for you in this chapter? What are you most proud of as a mom and why? Toot your own horn.

ACTIONS

Write down the goal you mentioned above along with 2-3 action steps and mark your progress as it happens. Tell your daughter what makes you proud of her.

AFFIRMATIONS

Repeat daily: I was built for motherhood. I can do hard things.

Chapter Two

WHAT'S REALLY GOING ON?

Dear mom,

I just wish you would let me explain/speak my mind more, not in a disrespectful way. I may not want to always wanna do everything your way, but I am willing to meet you halfway. But sometimes I don't feel heard. I also wish that you would not be so hard on me. I know that you want the best for me but being so hard on me is not really helping. It honestly makes it more stressful. It would also help if you just gave me a little bit more freedom. I'm a teenager now and I'm not a little kid anymore. Yeah maybe I'm not responsible enough or I make mistakes, but maybe if you just loosen up, you would see that I actually am responsible and I can do what I am supposed to do. You just have to trust me. I love you.

Your daughter,
Alissa, 15

Marvin Gaye said it best a long time ago - What's goin' on? (Look him up if he is before your time.) I don't need to tell you that times have changed. With the increase in social media pressure, FOMO (Fear Of Missing Out), YOLO (You Only Live Once) and other acronyms that confuse us, it is hard to keep up. Easy access to information, the changing of standards and values, the rise of new religious sects and cults, the push for individuality and autonomy, digital learning and ever-changing technology, have all affected the way we do things in this society. We cannot rely on the old way of doing things and how our parents taught us to do things because most of those suggestions don't apply anymore.

THE FACTS

Times are a changin'. There is an increase in sexual freedom and expression, the notion that people can basically do what they want to do, a lack of respect for authority, total obsession with selfies and looking good, blatant hatred and bullying and an influx of opinions - everybody has one and they're not afraid to share it. Change, not all bad, can be embraced or rejected. But it definitely has to be addressed. Because of this, mothers must change the way they approach their pre-teen and teenage daughters. We have to be more aware of what they do, who and what they listen to, and how they react to certain situations they experience.

Teens spend about nine hours a day on some type of media (CNN). The average American is inundated with between 4 and

10 thousand images a day (GradSchool.com). Between computers, cell phones, television, magazines and books, it can be very difficult to process all this information on a daily basis. This is what you are competing with moms. I will be the first to say, it will not be easy. The tremendous focus and attention on body image and self-esteem in the media has made the most beautiful "perfect" girl think she's ugly. Forty seven percent of girls ages 11-21 believe the way they look holds them back, and two-thirds of those ages 17 and up think they are not pretty enough. (Girlguiding UK's 2016 Girls' Attitudes Survey)

THE STRUGGLE IS REAL

I believe my daughter is gorgeous. Not only because she's my daughter, but also by society's standards. She's lighter skinned with gorgeous eyes, a perfect nose and nice full lips. She has an eye for style and is smart and well spoken. However, she had problems with self-esteem and how she looked. Honestly, I didn't always understand it, but I also find this very common as I talk to girls who check all of society's beauty boxes but are still insecure about their appearance.

Most young girls get up every day and find fault with something in their appearance, even though they may be totally beautiful or gorgeous. Because I believe my daughter is gorgeous, I used to struggle sometimes and wonder why she felt inadequate about her body or her appearance in some way. I used to think every girl wanted what she had. But I had to put myself in her shoes and figure out what she was looking at, paying attention to and comparing herself to that made her feel like she needed to improve in some area. **MAJOR KEY: Put yourself in your daughter's shoes and see things from her perspective and become familiar with what's going on in today's society.** Don't put your head in the sand. Don't say I don't know how to use social media. Learn how to use it. Know what Snapchat, Tumbler, Discord, and Telegram are. This is for your own benefit so you can be informed and know what's going on. We have to know what our daughters are struggling with so we can know how to help them.

COMPARISON IS THE THIEF OF JOY

We live in the age of comparison. Many of our daughters are comparing themselves to society's standards. I saw this practically every day as a teacher. I had students who despised their hair or looks, which I considered beautiful. I once taught at a school that was 75% Hispanic. The girls were absolutely gorgeous. Lots of them had the kind of skin that most people tan for - beautiful, brown and flawless. They had the kind of long, soft, curly hair that most people buy (wigs) and dream of having. And yet these girls in all their glory, still hated things about themselves. Every day I would listen to them criticize things they didn't like about their appearance - their weight, the coarseness of their hair, the brownness of their skin, their noses or anything they could find to discredit themselves.

Once during a conversation in our Girl Talk group, some of them mentioned, "I hate my hair." I asked, "Why do you hate your hair?" They explained it was hard to manage because it was long, coarse and took a lot of work to do. And I said wow, people are paying hundreds of dollars for hair just like yours. While it may take a lot to do, it just fits you so perfectly. But I also wondered where this hatred for their natural beauty came from. I found out that it stemmed mainly from who they were comparing themselves to. They were usually comparing themselves to white women with straight hair, skinny noses and bodies, who the media deemed gorgeous, such as the Kim Kardasians and Beyonces of the world.

African American girls have always struggled with hair issues because kinky, coarse hair was "not acceptable or attractive" to the masses. And while I am overjoyed that the natural hair movement has taken off and seems to be thriving and instilling pride in African American girls, I can't believe this is still a conversation we need to continually have. But this is what's going on with our daughters.

Be understanding when your daughter says she does not fit in and pay attention to what she is comparing herself to that makes her feel that way. Because trust me, it's something. And momma, please make sure it's not you. We are going to address that more in the next chapter, but how you treat yourself and speak to yourself about your body image and appearance is a mirror to your daughter. She is watching and learning. Are you treating yourself with kindness, grace, acceptance and love? Are you constantly bad-mouthing yourself or complaining about your weight and appearance? Look at how you treat yourself and the words you speak to yourself and make sure your words and actions are positive because your daughters are watching.

These shocking statistics confirm what I saw daily in the girls I worked with as mentor and educator.

- Only 4% of women around the world consider themselves beautiful (up from 2% in 2004)
- Only 11% of girls globally are comfortable describing themselves as 'beautiful'
- 72% of girls feel tremendous pressure to be beautiful
- 80% of women agree that every woman has something about her that is beautiful, but do not see their own beauty
- More than half of women globally (54%) agree that when it comes to how they look, they are their own worst beauty critic (Statistics from the Dove Beauty Research Group - www.dove.com)

Can you relate? I know I can. We are constantly bombarded with unrealistic images which is why being aware of what is really going on in your daughter's life and having these conversations is so important. Because of the changes in society and what society now looks like compared to when we were growing up, we have to approach things differently than the way our parents approached things with us, and even differently than you may have approached things with an older daughter. These are rapidly changing times and the role models, actresses and singers our daughters look up to don't resemble the ones we looked up to as teenagers. They are certainly wearing less clothing.

AWARENESS IS KEY

As parents, we need to stay on top of things, and while privacy has its place, we have to remember our calling is to guide our daughters through this life. Start early and be consistent. Stay vigilant and aware of what is going on in the lives of young people so you can effectively connect with your daughter. It's not being nosey; it's being a parent. I believe every parent has a charge to raise a child in the way they should go according to healthy values and standards. Girls want effective and authentic communication, preferably with their mothers. Life does not just happen. Moms, we have the power to influence what our daughters watch, know, understand about life, and even who they look up to. I believe mothers still have the greatest influence on the lives of teenage girls.

Be aware of what's going on in society. Be aware of the social media channels and people your daughter follow. Be aware of the celebrities they follow. Be aware of who their friends are. Be aware of their favorite TV shows and why they like them. Be aware of who they listen to, as far as music is concerned. Be aware of who they listen to as far as advice is concerned. Be aware of what they're feeling about school and why they feel that way. You have to make a conscious effort to be involved in your daughter's life even if she doesn't want you to. Because at the end of the day, you want that authentic connection.

CHAPTER CONCLUSION

Not only should you be aware, but also be prepared to do it differently than how you were parented if necessary. It is so easy to say, this is how I was taught and so that's how I'm going to parent because that's our default. Sometimes we do the same exact things that our moms did, even though we didn't like it, because it's our default. It's very subconscious. And if we don't make a conscious effort to do something differently, then our daughter will wind up the same way that we wound up whether good or not so good. So being open to learning something new and doing it differently is a key factor to improving and having authentic communication and connection with your daughters. Make the decision today to find out what's going on in society, your daughter's generation, and in your daughter's life. Knowing will help you connect on a deeper level.

QUESTIONS

Who did you talk to about hot topics as a teen and why? What made you talk to them?

ACTIONS

Find out who your daughter respects, listens to and goes to for advice. Ask her what she likes most about this person. No judgment here. You are just getting to know her better. What social media channels does she use? Familiarize yourself with them.

AFFIRMATION

I am open and willing to learn new things about my daughter without judgment.

NOW WE'RE TALKING

Most Popular Social Media Apps And Sites Used By Teens

- **Discord:** *A voice-over-IP (VOIP) app that allows users to video chat with others, private message, and join, create, or participate in public and private chat rooms. This app is often used by players to chat with each other while playing videogames.*

- **Houseparty:** *A group video chat and social networking app that allows up to eight people to video chat at once in a "room."*

- **Instagram:** *A photo and video sharing and networking site that connects users through other social networking sites (e.g., Facebook).*

- **Snapchat:** *A photo messaging app that allows for sharing pictures and short videos that are intended to be erased shortly after delivery.*

- **TikTok:** *An app that allows users to create and share their own videos where they lip-synch, sing, dance, or just talk.*

- **YouTube:** *A video sharing platform that allows users*

Information provided by: https://www.stopbullying.gov/cyberbullying/social-media-apps-sites-commonly-used-children-teens.

Please visit the site for a complete list.

Chapter Three

WHAT'S YOUR STORY?

Dear Mom,

I love you so much and I appreciate all of the sacrifices you have made for me. I know that I can be a bit of a handful, but hey, I think I turned out pretty good.

As your daughter, I've had to learn so many lessons on my own. We both know our communication skills weren't the strongest, and you have always expressed to me how hard of a time you have finding the right words to say. Because of this, I grew up thinking in a mode of perfection, unsure if the next thing that comes out of my mouth would make sense or come off the right way. Thus, creating a life of reservation and my navigation of youth trapped within the mind. It became difficult to express myself to you about particular things, especially sensitive topics. I was so unsure about how you would respond, or if you would respond at all. I ended up having to resort to my own devices for this clarification. Thank God for the gift of discernment.

I've noticed a shift in your communication and recognize your growth. We have both evolved into new women and have a beautiful patience with each other. I am stepping into this new chapter of life as an adult and pray our communication grows. Thank you. Again, I love you so much and I wouldn't trade our relationship for the world.

Love,
Zoe, 20

Before we begin talking about how to listen to our daughter's story, let us first consider our own story. Our stories, how we were spoken to, raised, our birth order, environment, how we were nurtured and our relationship with our parents all affect how we communicate and deal with our children. It is all connected. Your story of growing up and learning about your body, identity, self-worth and the types of relationships you had will impact and dictate how you will approach these same issues and topics with your own daughter. The relationship you have with your mother is also very critical and has to be examined, because more likely than not, that relationship is probably being perpetuated whether you realize it or not. So, we must make conscious efforts to first look at our story and become self-aware of how we process information. If you're satisfied with how you and your mom communicated and you evolved into a secure, confident, brave adult, use those gems and share them with your daughter and every girl you know.

But if you are not satisfied with how you and your mom communicated, prepare to do something differently. I realize that this process may be difficult for you, mom, but if you truly want to foster a better, more connected relationship with your daughter, doing the hard work is necessary. And we already declared that we can do hard things. An added benefit is that you will be healed in the process as well.

LET'S TAKE A TRIP

Do you remember how you learned about your period, sex, boys, consent or who you are? If so, take yourself on a journey back to those times - adolescence. Close your eyes and take a trip down memory lane. Do you remember how you first learned about your period? How did you feel? What do you wish would have happened that didn't? Remember the first boy you liked? How old were you? Did you tell anyone? Why or why not? How did your mother communicate her values to you? What was her tone like? Did you feel like you had a safe space? Why or why not? Were you afraid to speak your truth? I know those are a lot of questions, but I want you to sit with yourself for a moment and process the answers. Jot some notes down if you feel led.

I didn't realize how traumatic my relationship was with my mother until I began parenting my two children. Boy did it open my eyes. By default, I did the exact same things she did. She was overly critical. I was overly critical. She spanked. I spanked. She yelled. I yelled. She had antiquated ways about how children should behave and so did I. "Children should be seen and not heard." "Spare the rod and spoil the child." "A child should stay in a child's place." "Stop crying, before I give you something to cry about." "Because I said so." Does any of this sound familiar?

CONFRONT YOUR STORY

These are the messages many of us received and we didn't like them at the time and guess what? Our daughters don't either. These messages literally silenced us in a place where we should have felt seen, heard and understood most - home. I won't even begin to talk about religious conditioning. I am a true believer in God and Jesus Christ, but some of the scare tactics our parents and the church used to make sure we didn't "sin," are still haunting some of us today. Religious conditioning made me totally suppress my sexuality. (That's my next book.) Fortunately, while my children were still young (4-5), I recognized these unhealthy patterns and began correcting them. But I had to confront my story. I had to examine my triggers and why I parented the way I did, and so do you. **MAJOR KEY: Confront your story and examine your triggers so you can be the mom you want to be.**

I still cry today sometimes when I retell this story. One day my daughter, who was about 4-5 at the time, was misbehaving in public at the Boys and Girls Club where they played while I worked. I pulled her to the side and disciplined her by smacking her on the side of her head, harder than I intended. I immediately regretted it, and the look of fear and disappointment on her face was something I never wanted to see again. As a child, I was spanked and occasionally smacked across the head, so it was my default.

Naturally she began to cry, and I scooped her up and hugged her tightly apologizing profusely. Right then and there I realized that hitting while angry was abuse and I had to change. Although it was my default, I had the power to create a new reality and story for my family. And you do too. It was the wakeup call that I needed to change. I didn't want my children to be afraid of me. I loved them immensely and wanted them to feel love, not fear. While I knew I would have to discipline them at times, I realized at that moment that it didn't have to be physical. I didn't have to yell. I could discipline them calmly. More importantly, I realized that I didn't want to be that type of mom. I wanted them to grow up confident and learn how to manage their own behavior. After all, these were their formative years. They are learning how to do things, and I am their first and most important teacher.

So, my story was that I was spanked or popped for misbehaving, instead of being talked to and that had a direct effect on me. One of my triggers was being embarrassed in public. This is a no-no in the African American community. Whenever we went somewhere, my mother sternly warned, "Don't embarrass me!" When my daughter misbehaved, she embarrassed me and I reacted. I made it about me. I had to realize this and confront my behavior if I wanted it to change.

As I said before, being a single parent was extremely stressful and hard. The pressures of motherhood, balancing work, children and a household, and not having support during the journey accounted for my lack of patience at times. It was not an excuse, just my reality. But I had to create a new reality if I wanted things to be different for my children. Therefore, knowing your story is key. You can't change what you don't acknowledge. Hurt people, hurt people, and I use the term hurt very broadly. This was part of my story that I wanted to change. But I wouldn't have been able to change it if I didn't recognize it. We have to look at what we've been through and how it affected us, so we don't repeat behaviors that no longer serve us.

As you think about who you want your daughter to be: strong, smart, bold, well adjusted, etc., you also have to think about what role you will play in ensuring that those characteristics are transferred. How will you encourage your daughter to be strong, bold, and love herself? Again, a mother's influence is particularly significant in teenage girls' lives. According to USA Today, mothers have the biggest influence on girls' body image. Our daughters are watching what we do and say. Pay attention to the story you are writing everyday with your words and actions. This is the book your daughter reads daily. What you are telling yourself, you are also telling your daughter.

Caveat here. In reminiscing about your story, especially difficult parts of your childhood, please be aware of your triggers and parts of you that are not healed. A therapist is strongly recommended if you still have some trauma to work through. Helping yourself will help your daughter. It's sort of like what the flight attendant tells you during the flight speech: In case of an emergency and loss of oxygen, please put your mask on first before helping someone else. Knowing and dealing with your story first, equips you to react in an appropriate way to your daughter's story.

RETHINK YOUR ACTIONS

After looking at my poor parenting patterns, I made the decision to confront my story head on and to not be afraid to change. Older generations of African Americans generally are not fans of time out and other seemingly "ineffective" methods of discipline, like talking to your child, counting to 10 or grounding. But I tried and learned new methods to encourage my children to self-correct and manage unwanted behaviors.

The first thing I tried was asking more questions. People in general do not ask enough questions or the right questions. In Chapter 8, I will delve into this more. Ask questions for clarity, understanding, redirection and answers. The right questions help you understand intent and motivation. Asking questions eliminates assumptions and ambiguity and allows you to respond the correct way because now you fully understand what is going on. In using the example with my young daughter, here are the questions I could have asked: "What were you doing?" (Clarity) "Why did you do that?" (understanding) "Why did you think that was the right thing to do?" (intent/understanding) "What could you have done instead? (redirection) "What could you do next time that happens?" (intrinsic motivation and self-regulation) "How can I help you do this the next time it happens?" (support and connection) By the way, don't accept "I don't know" as an answer, and give them time to think between each question. Yes, it takes a bit more time. Yes, you will have to be calm. Yes, you have to watch your body language. But isn't this so much better than what I actually did?

Another thing I tried was active listening. I will mention this in more detail in Chapter 8 also. Active listening is removing all distractions, leaning in and really hearing what the person is saying. You are not thinking about responding, just understanding. Your teenage daughter may not know how to verbalize everything she's thinking but guide her in communicating her thoughts effectively. You are teaching her how to be an effective communicator and this is a skill that she can use throughout her life. Give her prompts if needed, like "You feel this way because…, You wanted to do that because… You were thinking that…"

These two methods alone were a game changer for me. I learned to listen to my children despite what I was told by my mother and in spite of cultural norms. Children do need to be seen and heard and what they think and say is important. In addition to those things, I found out what motivated each of my children to self-correct. For my son, it was grounding. He loved to play outside with his friends. It was the highlight of his day.

Grounding him and not letting him ride his bike or go out with friends, changed his behavior almost immediately. For my daughter, it was taking away things like television, toys or books. She found joy and pleasure in these things and when I denied her these things, she was motivated to change her behavior.

Grounding didn't work for my daughter, because she pretty much liked being alone. Taking away things didn't work for my son, because his true joy came from being with others. You have to know your daughter and what motivates her. These strategies didn't work every single time and they didn't always work perfectly. But my new approach to discipline drastically changed the dynamic of our relationship for the better. Children do need discipline. As the Bible says in Hebrews 12:11, "No discipline seems pleasant at the time, but painful. Later, however, it produces a harvest of righteousness and peace for those who have been trained by it." Having disciplined children produces peace. Amen? My children and I both found a better way, but I had to confront my story and rethink my actions.

KNOW THYSELF

Whether your daughter trusts you or not depends on the way you react when she tells you her secrets and desires. When you ask your daughter to share information with you, she's assuming you really want to know. Sometimes parents ask for information and when they get what they asked for, they're shocked. Be prepared for what she might tell you. It might not be what you want to hear. More importantly, be aware of your reaction. If your daughter shares something important to her with you and you react angrily, judgmentally, uninterested or in any way that makes her feel small or unimportant, this will be her LAST TIME telling you anything. Trust me when I say this. Girls often tell me that this is the number 1 reason why they don't share information with their mothers.

Your trauma may cause you to react adversely to your daughter if she told you about an experience she had that caused trauma for you. For example, if you have experienced any kind of sexual abuse, and your daughter tells you that someone touched her inappropriately, of course are going to be angry. Not only because someone violated your daughter, but also because it brings alive your own unhealed trauma. This trigger may cause you to shut down, act irrationally, or maybe even become embarrassed. Since you are triggered and upset, you may not be in the best position to listen or help your daughter.

So, knowing your story and dealing with your stuff first will help you show up authentically. But most of all, we just need to be self-aware. We need to be aware of what triggers us. If you come from a strict religious background, there will probably be a lot of things that trigger you, and you must decide if you want to stick to those beliefs or create new ones for your family. Self-awareness is your friend. Don't be afraid of who you are because we usually don't confront what we are afraid of.

I have a friend who was molested as a young girl. She told her mother who said it was her fault for being fast, and basically didn't believe her. My friend began to believe that it was her fault. After all, her mother had said so! She and her mother have a very strained relationship to this day and my friend is in her 60s. But here's the kicker, my friend became an abuser as well. The only thing I can think of that would make her feel that it was alright to inappropriately touch another person, was believing that it was the other person's fault. Just like she had been taught. Do you see the damage that can be done if you don't get your healing? Momma, I can't emphasize enough that this is important work. Know your story and get help if you need to.

CHAPTER CONCLUSION

What was communication like in your family? What would you have liked for it to be like? Think about the questions I asked in the beginning of this chapter. Those are some of the questions that you may not have been able to talk to your mother about. Examining your story unlocks the key to how you help build your daughter's story. Do you want her story to be the same as yours?

What I would have liked to happen in my own life was for my mother to sit down with her daughters and tell us that she was a safe space. She had five children, four of which were girls. She had a tough childhood, growing up in the 1940s and 1950s, where women were not valued, and were often the subjects of sexual abuse as she was. Sharing more of her story and what she learned from it would have helped us understand what is good and what is not good. Every single one of her daughters were sexually abused. There was no safe space to discuss what we went through, and no place for vulnerability and understanding. Instead, all of that was brushed under the rug and I didn't find out about my mother's sexual abuse until I was an adult. I have never shared with my mother about my sexual abuse from a neighbor. This is how not dealing with your story can play out. How this manifested in my own life is me having very little trust and security in men. I didn't feel safe around them. This caused me to be very guarded and suspicious, which killed connection with even the greatest man. I am still working through this in therapy. I would have liked my mother to sit down and just talk to us and let us know that she comes with no judgment, and she understands what we girls have to endure because I think deep down she did, but she never let us know that. I know many of you have similar stories.

If we don't examine our past, are we really equipped to help our daughters in the future? If you don't get healed or seek help in the areas you need to, connection to your daughter may not be possible and it could be the reason why some of you are not connecting now. So that is my encouragement. That is really what I want you to do. I want you to take that self-inventory. I want you to take a trip down memory lane and think about what you learned and what you didn't learn, what you would have liked to learn and see how some of those things could affect you when communicating with your daughter.

Now, as you explore your story, you will have to decide what you're willing to share and what you're not willing to share depending upon your daughter's age. You won't share everything with her at one time. You might give her little pieces of it at a time and that is okay. As she grows up, you might share a little more. You also want to make sure that you don't use scare tactics because something bad or negative may have happened to you. You don't want to make it seem like it happens to everyone and make her so afraid of everybody that she can't enjoy life or just be a girl.

We all know that the world is generally not a safe place for women. There are many misogynistic people and ideologies seeking to keep us in "our place." Crimes against women are at an all-time high, and as far as society is concerned, we are still second-class citizens. You get a tougher jail sentence for abandoning an animal (a felony punishable for up to 5 years) than for violating a domestic violence order of protection (6-18 months).

Despite this, we want our children to live life to the fullest because the Creator gave us this life and we have to live it. We can't live it inside the house being afraid of everything and everybody. We must talk about these things and allow our biases, our trauma, our hard times to be exposed so we can heal.

Do you expose everything to your daughter? Absolutely not. You don't want your daughter to become your therapist or sounding board. Enlist the help of a professional therapist or trusted friend if you need to, so you can show up as a helper and ally for your daughter. But first you must operate in self-awareness. Be brave and get the help that you need. I know you can do it. After this chapter, you might have to take a little time to just set up that therapy appointment even if you didn't grow up with traumatic experiences. Therapy is good for many reasons including just exploring some of the reasons why you feel the way you do, or why you do the things you do. Some free or almost free therapy resources are listed in the Appendix.

QUESTION

Think about how your growing up story helped or hurt the adult you are today. What would you have liked to discuss with your mother and why didn't you?

ACTION

Examining your Triggers - Let's examine some things that may trigger you. Grab a sheet of paper and a pencil. I am going to list some words. Please move to a space where you can say these words aloud. After you say the word aloud, jot down some thoughts that immediately come to mind.

WHAT'S YOUR STORY?

Grab a sheet of paper and a pencil, or use the space on the next page.

READY

Sex, masturbation, love, self-worth, identity, diet, gay, touch, safety, consent, dating, puberty, trust. mother.

If you spot any triggers during this exercise, please get the help of a therapist or trusted friend to talk it out. Triggers may look like becoming angry, crying, getting chills, getting a headache, feeling shame, shutting down or silence, frustration, turning to something that comforts you or blaming others.

AFFIRMATION

I cannot change the past, but I can change the future for my daughter's sake, and I will.

Notes

Chapter Four

Unlearning

Dear Mama,

In retrospect, I can see all the ways you loved me in the way you knew how. But mama, I have to tell you I didn't feel loved during my childhood. I needed time and nurturing from you. I needed you to hug me and show me affection. I needed you to take interest in me as a person and come to at least one of my basketball games or ask me about school. I needed intimate conversations with you to discuss how life was so confusing to me. Or conversations about my hopes and dreams. I needed you to say I love you and make eye contact with me and tell me I was beautiful. I needed kind words and less harshness. I needed you to touch me – pat my hand, rub my arm, kisses on the cheek, warm hugs. Dear God, I needed touch.

I remember when I got chickenpox as a little girl. I had a large pox sore on my back. It was awful - a mixture of itching and pain, and I was confined to days of lying on my stomach in misery. But the sickness was bittersweet, because you nursed me. You were gentle. I remember you periodically coming into the bedroom and rubbing the calamine lotion on my back. I longed for that gentle, loving mother's touch for many years after I recovered. Mama, I know that you love me. As a teenager, I just wish you were able to express that love in a way I could feel.

Dara, 42

Now that you have examined your story. You may realize that there are some things you will have to unlearn to foster effective communication with your daughter. What did you discover? What did your parents, family members, support system or church teach you that you realized was not true or didn't align with how you desired to live your life? Let's face it, as we were growing up, things were taught to us by significant people in our lives that were not helpful. Many of our moms had experiences with their own parents that they transferred to us, even though those experiences were not positive. We, in turn, transferred or are transferring those words and experiences to our daughters. We do it because it's what we know. And you can only give what you know until you decide to learn something different. Even with love, you can't give what you don't have. **MAJOR KEY: Be willing to unlearn those experiences that you felt didn't serve you and to take the chance to relearn new ways of communicating.**

In my years of working with girls and young women, I discovered there are some common recurring themes we must unlearn. If we don't, the sentiments will be transferred to our daughters. UNLEARN:

1. **You are not enough.** You are not pretty enough, thin enough, social enough, quiet enough, sexy enough…ENOUGH!!! Social media, television, ads, spouses, partners, parents, teachers, hell…everyone sends women messages daily that we need something else. We are constantly bombarded with images to lose weight, change our hair, be a boss, earn the bacon, cook the bacon, clean the house, provide good lovin' and the like. And as women, we listen. We are constantly trying to improve something. We reign in the self-help category.

   While this in and of itself is not bad, it is extremely taxing to continually feel that our best efforts are not enough. If you don't want your daughter to deal with this on the home front at least, unlearn that. Mom, you are enough and don't let anyone tell you otherwise. Be your authentic self, whether you snort when you laugh, prefer sneakers to high heels, or want to be a stay-at-home mom over working outside the home. BE YOU. Because embracing who you truly are will encourage your daughter to do the same.

2. **Feeling guilty.** This was a big one for me. Raise your hand if you have made mistakes as a mom. I see the hand of every mom in the world. There is no handbook for this and if there

is, it cannot possibly accommodate every person and situation. Guilt is the unhappy feeling you get when you've done something wrong, or you think you've done something wrong. Most of the time, it's the latter. We think we are supposed to parent according to some standard, and when we don't, we feel guilty and beat ourselves up. We may even overcompensate by allowing our daughters to do things we wouldn't normally allow them to do because we feel guilty. For example, sometimes when a father is not present, we overspend and cater to our daughter's every whim to make up for the fact that dad is not around. We take on that guilt and try to make it better with the latest sneakers, purse or jeans. But we shouldn't feel guilty because we are there doing the work of raising our daughters.

Sometimes our parents made us feel guilty, or they made comments that were not helpful like, "Are you wearing that?" Maybe they were overly critical and every time we had an opinion, they had one. Sometimes, they just didn't give us the support or encouragement we needed. I know there have been times when I was critical of what my daughter wore or opinions she had. Criticism was something I picked up from my mother, who was very critical of me. I had to recognize that I was critical in order to acknowledge it and unlearn it. How did I unlearn it? I stopped giving my opinion or commenting unless it was asked for, and then I made the decision to respond how I would have wanted my mother to respond to me.

Try it. Insert gratitude here. I'll pause here to thank my daughter for teaching me how to treat her. Because I allowed her to have a voice, she told me how she felt judged, and it hurt my heart to know it was because of my words. That was never my intention and I know it's not yours. Unlearn feeling guilty.

3. **Silencing our voices** - Outdated principles taught by our parents and other adults in our family from older generations are not applicable or helpful with the present generation. Saying things like children should be seen and not heard, or power tripping and saying, "Because I said so," like our grandmothers said, will not help you develop an authentic relationship with your daughter. These messages silence voices. They communicate to your daughter that what she has to say is not important and you don't want to hear it. Today's teens want to know why. Something we would not dare ask growing up. But that doesn't work well with this generation. Understanding why helps today's youth process the intention of the message. When they don't understand why, they are more likely to rebel because they do not understand the purpose of the message.

As a teacher, I often had students ask me why we had to learn something like proper grammar, for example. I explained to them that good grammar and proper punctuation helps others understand what they have to say. I would use this popular example when talking about the importance of punctuation:

"Let's eat Grandma." vs "Let's eat, Grandma." The first sentence implies that you want to eat your grandmother. While the second sentence is telling Grandma that you are ready to eat. Once students understood this concept, and if clarity and being understood was important to them, they then had a reason to use proper grammar because they saw its purpose. The same is true when you are explaining things to your daughter. Saying "Because I said so," doesn't communicate purpose and intent, therefore giving your daughter no reason to obey other than fear. Welcome the whys and be prepared to give your daughter answers that communicate purpose and intent.

Previous generations failed to hold a man accountable if he was inappropriate to a female in word or deed. It wasn't talked about. Most of our grandmothers and mothers would just make excuses for Uncle Joe's bad behavior. They taught us by example that silence was the solution, instead of having a voice and speaking up. To this day some women are still suffering from the silence of those they trusted and those who failed to use their voices. In turn, teaching us not to use ours. Girls were even encouraged not to be too loud because men don't like women like that. I pray that women unlearn being silent about abuse in any form.

We need to review our past experiences to discover whether they are affecting how we communicate with our daughters now. Are we passing on the same ideas to our daughters and making them feel the same way we did at the time? Are we giving messages to our daughters that communicate that saying nothing is better than saying something? Teach your daughter that she has a voice and it deserves to be heard, respectfully.

4. **Comparison** - I could write a whole chapter on this one. Our obsession with social media and television comparisons is unnatural. We all looked up to certain television families, be it the one on the Cosby Show, Leave It to Beaver, This is Us or whatever we watched on TV that we idolized. But most of the time, the women in those series and the relationships they had didn't reflect real life. Women woke up looking perfect. They always smelled good. They performed stereotypical roles. And the further you go back, the worse it was. Yet, we desired to be like them. Why? Because that's what the media and society was telling us that women should be like. So, we began to compare ourselves to them, and when we didn't measure up, we started fixing ourselves.

What media mother did you idolize? Being cognizant of what we allow in our eye gate and ear gate is crucial. Constantly seeing women and girls who "have it all together," "slaying in every area" etc. messes with our psyche and we think, why am I not like that? What's wrong with me? Know what's important to you. Know your core values and stay aligned with them.

Core values are things that are important to you and they guide how you choose to live your life. For example, some of my core values are faith, family, fun, financial stability and friendship. I place these things at the top of my list when it comes to what I care about. I constantly monitor what I am watching, listening to or doing to make sure it aligns with my core values. What's important to you, will become important to your daughter. Living according to your core values allows you to eliminate things that are not aligned. Core values are what you want to teach your daughter. Communicate your core values, your family's core values and help her develop her own core values. This is important because when she comes across a person or idea, she can assess whether it aligns with her personal core values. This is an excellent gauge to take into her adult life. It will quickly help her assess situations and make good decisions. (See Appendix for Core Value Assessments)

5. **Religious conditioning** - I remember my church constantly teaching young girls to be modest by wearing skirts down to your ankles and shirts up to their necks. Doing otherwise meant you were "loose." Although I didn't take it that far, I was very aware of being modest. "You don't want to tempt men." THIS I had to unlearn. Dressing so that you feel good about yourself, or according to your own style, or wearing a skirt above your knees or shorts, does not make you a Jezebel. Don't men want attractive women? Besides, a man is responsible for his behavior, no matter how a girl/woman is dressed.

That should have been the complimentary message. But it was rarely mentioned.

Another thing we were always told in church is to aspire to be a Proverbs 31 woman. Don't even get me started with this one. Basically, the church's interpretation of this scripture is to do everything - work, take care of the house, husband and children, cook, clean - and be perfect. Impossible. (Slaps hand to forehead) The man's message was (not surprisingly) be the head of your household.

If you grew up religious, you may have a lot to unlearn. Not because what you learned was bad, but mainly because religious conditioning may be misaligned with who you want to be. Some women have been carrying around guilt and condemnation for years because of religious practices and beliefs. Raises hand. During my late 30s and early 40s, I realized a lot of what religion taught me was contrary to God's purpose for our individual and unique bodies and personalities. Let me emphasize that I make a very distinct difference between religion and relationship. Religion consists of rules and a way of doing things and can be void of relationship. The Pharisees were religious but didn't have a relationship with the Father. I don't want to go too deeply into this, but religion will keep you stuck and confused. Oftentimes there is a disconnect about what God intended and what a church teaches. People who grew up in certain faiths or became religious understand what I am talking about. All I can admonish without being too preachy, is to read and understand the entirety of the Bible and biblical history for yourself. If you really desire to know the truth, God will reveal it to you if you ask sincerely and in faith.

THE JOURNEY BEGINS WITH YOU

So here's where the work comes in mama. For some of you, it's going to take a lot of unlearning. For others, you've already begun the process without this book. Others, it may be just a few changes you need to make. But the journey is yours to take.

If you are a person of faith, begin there. I find this area to be the hardest to unlearn because some of us have had years of indoctrination. It took me many, many years to unlearn some of the misogynistic tenets taught by the church. Examine how your faith and the people you admired communicated about your identity, womanhood and femininity. If you feel stuck and don't quite know how to unlearn religious doctrines, a therapist or coach may be helpful.

The next place to look is at your own relationship with your mother. How did your mom handle her own journey into womanhood? Many of the things she felt and experienced were transferred to you in some way, consciously or unconsciously. Was she shunned for being too provocative or feminine? Did she grow up in a very strict, religious household? Did she grow up with constant criticism? Was she told to stay in a child's place? Were you? Did she have trust issues? Do you?

The final thing that must be examined is who you admire and why. Do you admire stay-at-home moms and think they have the ideal life being at home taking care of their kids and husband? Do you long for freedom from the 9-5 and desire to start your own business? Are you still waiting for your Cinderella story or think women should be meek, passive little princesses? Do you celebrate individuality, authenticity and non-traditional gender roles? How you view relationships, womanhood, sex, love, trust, etc. will all be transferred in a million tiny ways to your daughter.

I had to go on this womanhood journey myself and enlisted a coach to help me do so, because this is the stuff that no one teaches you - how to walk in your feminine power. I felt like I had to always fit in a mold, whether it was being a good straight A student, the daughter who didn't cause trouble, the faithful church girl or the virtuous woman. Trying to make my parents proud and happy and living up to society's standards of what a woman should be like, put out my fire. It smothered my authentic self. It made me hide my silliness, quirkiness, fierce determination, hopes and desires. I had to unlearn perfectionism and people pleasing. Women are constantly being put in a box with directions on how they are to look, think and behave. When I realized that I wasn't being my true and authentic self, I began taking steps to reclaim who I am and who I want to be. That's the journey you must take.

On my journey, I realized that my femininity and who I was as a woman is not something that I needed to suppress. God made us beautiful and wonderful. Some of us have been so repressed as women and taught not to feel like our true, authentic, sexy, sensual selves. We've been made to think or to believe that it's wrong and it's not. Women are shapely, curvaceous, sensual and feminine and that is not wrong or dirty. If we are not careful, we will communicate those thoughts to our daughters. In an attempt to protect them, we sometimes make them feel ashamed for how they look or how they feel. So we need new tools to communicate and help our daughters feel empowered in their femininity.

HOW YOU BUILD A HOUSE IS HOW IT STANDS

Be willing to unlearn what you need to, so you can live the life you desire and pave the way for your daughter to do the same. Listen, we are trying to change generations of misinformation and low self worth. If you are not willing to unlearn these things, you are setting your daughter up for the same poor communication or miscommunication that you had with your mother. Learn to build your house with open communication.

Refusing to unlearn and be open to understanding your daughter will bring a fast and heavy wedge between you two. Girls are struggling with real life, hard issues and emotional stressors. Do we want them to navigate these things on their own? Some have fallen into depression, self-harm, smoking or other negative behaviors just to cope because they can't talk to their parents because their parents are too close minded. Please don't be that parent. If your daughter comes to you and says, "Hey mom, I think I like girls." Be open to understanding what she is talking about, even if it is contrary to what you believe. Probe further, ask questions, understand her why, get help if you need to, but most of all show love. Learn to build your house with understanding.

If your daughter comes to you and asks you a question about sex, please don't chastise her or God forbid call her names like whore or fast, because you're closing the door to connection. Asking a question about sex does not mean she wants to engage in sex. After all, at one time you were interested in knowing about sex. Open that door for discussion and see what she means by sex. Sometimes teenagers don't even fully understand all that sex entails. It is not just a physical act, it's an emotional one also. They think it's kissing, or they might think it's oral stimulation, or they might think it's penetration. We don't really know until we ask questions and open up those conversations so that we can understand what they mean.

In national surveys conducted by the National Campaign to Prevent Teen and Unplanned Pregnancy, teens report that their parents have the greatest influence on their decisions about sex - more than friends, siblings or the media. In this same survey, most teens also say making decisions about delaying sex would be easier if they could talk openly and honestly with their parents.

(Albert B., 2012, The National Campaign to Prevent Teen and Unplanned Pregnancy from http://thenationalcampaign.org/resource/onevoice-2012) Learn to build your house with open doors.

If you were shut out and felt unheard when you asked questions about sex, unlearn that and adopt an attitude of openness and acceptance. Mom, our daughters' feelings are real, just like yours were. I know this is just not about sex, it's about everything. Not feeling attractive and loved by others accounts for a lot of the self-esteem issues women go through. Are we pretty enough? Are we tall enough? Are we light enough? Is our hair good enough? Are our boobs big enough? Is our body small enough? Am I funny enough? A lot of that is questioned because of how we relate to men. So that's why I'm using a lot of examples related to dating and relationships. But all of the things discussed in this chapter shapes our identity and who we are as young women, which then affects how we relate to men and women and even to ourselves. So we must be willing as mothers to unlearn some of the negativity and shame associated with feeling sexual and vibrant as a woman.

I think we need to unlearn how we view our daughters and their feelings. Sometimes we shut down how they feel and when we do, they shut down, and that could go on for many, many years. These girls will become women, and when they have repressed too much of who they are for so long, it takes a toll on their self-esteem and self-worth. This is why we have grown, adult women still dealing with their girl issues. Because they were never dealt with. When girls have low self-worth or don't understand who they are and where they fit in, they begin doing things to overcompensate for the lack of self-esteem and self-worth. Things like giving too much too soon, or not requiring a man to step up to the plate, or accepting people who abuse them, or not trusting anyone, or being promiscuous because they just want love. You see how important this is. It can be a vicious cycle. If we don't unlearn some things and adopt a new mindset, it can be extremely dangerous for not only your daughter, but for future generations. Learn to build your house with the next generation in mind.

CHAPTER CONCLUSION

You can become who you want to be to bond with your daughter. You can become the expert because you have been there. Who do you need to be, mom? Do you need to be more confident in who you are? Do you need to gain more information to help you feel comfortable about having difficult conversations? Do you need to see a therapist to help you unlearn some things? Do you need to forgive someone? Be open to unlearning and relearning so that we can help our daughters be successful on this growing up journey.

Allow me to re-emphasize why this is super important. How you experienced growing up and growing pains probably didn't have to be that way 90 percent of the time. Many of the problems you experienced as a young girl growing up probably could have been resolved with a conversation. It probably could have been resolved with your parents being willing to unlearn some things and relearn some new things. They probably could have been resolved with you being free and feeling free to open up and trust someone enough to talk about the things that you wanted to talk about without feeling shame or condemnation. Am I right? I know for a fact that some of my adult issues would be non-existent if I would have had a safe space to share what I was going through as a teenage girl and allowed to feel my emotions instead of suppressing them. Moms, it doesn't have to be this way. You have the power to change the narrative and how you communicate with your daughter through unlearning.

QUESTIONS

What do you have to unlearn? Sit with yourself for a moment and write it down? What do you need to do to unlearn this? Be specific.

ACTIONS

Choose one thing from what you wrote above. Now do it. Take the action steps needed to unlearn what you wrote down.

AFFIRMATION

I am willing to be who I need to be and do what I need to do for the sake of a better relationship with my daughter.

Chapter Five

MINDSET MATTERS

Dear Mom,

I am grateful for our relationship, but I do wish you would have been more open and understanding about some things. I wish I could have felt comfortable discussing certain parts of my life or ideas with you without feeling judged or dismissed. I know you grew up old school, but this is the new school and you have to understand that I go through different things than you did and we handle things differently today. It's ok to learn and be open to new things. I learned a lot on my own, but I wish I didn't have to.

I love you,
Daniella, 22

Moms, I have no doubt in my mind that you can do this. But you do have to examine and possibly change your mindset. You must be willing to make the necessary shifts in bridging the gaps between you and your daughter. You need to be willing to do something you may have never done before. Unlearning begins with shifting your mindset so you can effectively break down walls and communicate effectively with your daughter.

YOUR TEEN DAUGHTER WANTS TO TALK TO YOU

First, let's shift our mindset about teenagers not wanting to talk to us. They do. They tell me so. Society pegs teenagers as rude, disobedient and unruly. They can be, and so can adults. We've all had our moments, let's face it. I refused to accept the fact that my own teenagers and the teenagers I taught would be what's considered the status quo. I expected them to talk to me politely, be obedient and to listen. Since I set the expectation, that's what happened. You must expect that your daughter wants to talk to you despite her actions.

When you assume that your daughter will react a certain way, you close the door to seeing who she truly is. When you assume that she doesn't want to talk to you, you won't make the effort to build a connection. Go in with the premise that she does want to talk to you, and not only that, she does want to listen to what you have to say. Expect her to be honest and be ok with that. You may hear some things you don't want to, but as long as it's respectful, be open. This is one of the sentiments I hear most from teenage girls. "I tried to talk to my mother, but when I answered her question honestly, she said I was being disrespectful." Moms, we have to really understand that our daughters look up to us and admire us for so many things. When they share their hearts with us, we must receive what they are saying in the spirit that they are saying it. Your daughter may not have all the right words but hear her heart.

KEEP YOUR STRUGGLES TO YOURSELF

My mindset was jacked up about a lot of things. I struggled with trusting people, especially men, because I had never seen healthy relationships with men in my childhood. In my family men weren't trusted and couldn't be counted on. Needless to say, I struggled with that as an adult. I had to be careful not to let my mindset about men be transferred to my daughter. My struggle was my struggle, not my daughter's. If you don't recognize this, you will embed and transfer a lot of your beliefs to her, as my mother did with me and my sisters.

My parents were separated when I was about 2 or 3 years old. While my mother did not openly speak ill of my father, I never witnessed cordial, loving exchanges between them. As I got older, I learned that he was somebody that could not be trusted to keep child support current or take care of his kids the way we needed to be cared for. He couldn't be relied on to keep his word to pick us up at a certain time or attend our school events as promised. While, as a child, I continually gave him the benefit of the doubt, the adult in me filed his name under: People I can't trust to show up for me. While he was present sometimes and still my hero (because I so wanted him to be), I felt that this was typical male behavior. It wasn't, but that was all I knew at the time. Let me say that there are plenty of wonderful fathers out there. This was my reality, not my daughter's. But strangely enough, she saw the same behaviors in her father. Go figure. I was always careful to speak well of her father and men in general, because I realized that she probably would adopt my actions and attitudes.

I also learned from my older sisters' relationships that men could not be trusted. They would often talk about their boyfriends cheating or not doing things they were supposed to do. Even in my own relationships, I settled for less, because I expected less. I felt like any minute the ball was going to drop and any good that he did was going to end. Better was not coming. I didn't have high or positive expectations of men because I figured they were just going to disappoint me anyway so I might as well accept what I had. Although this was my perception, again I was careful not to project that on to my daughter. I went to therapy y'all. I didn't want my struggle to be her struggle.

WHAT'S ON YOUR MIND

My body image, rejection from people I loved, conflicting messages from the church, the media's objectification of women and imperfect family relationships all played a factor in me having a warped mindset about my femininity and who I was as a woman.

Our daughters have or will experience some of the same limited mindsets from these same sources. Knowing how you think, what you believe, your standards, values and boundaries will help you make mindset shifts where needed so you can help her navigate her mindset challenges when they arise.

By examining your mindset, you pave the way to make radical and real change for your daughter. Your willingness to shift your mindset and invite open and honest communication can lead to generations of change for your family line and for young women in general. I am going to keep repeating this point because it's important. In this society, women are constantly questioning who they are and what they have to offer.

We seem to have the most issues with self-esteem and self-identity and where we belong in this world. We have struggled for relevance since the beginning of time and through it all continue to rise to the challenges we face. To reverse the way that we look at ourselves and make it better for our daughters to look at themselves with bold, fierce, unapologetic love, we have to change this narrative, and that begins with changing your mindset. If we do not change our mindset about communication with our daughters, weight, body image, self-esteem, self-identity and self-love, we will continue to repeat unhealthy cycles and have the same generational issues that women have had for centuries. I most certainly don't want that for your child and I know you don't either. So managing your mind is critical.

GROW YOUR MINDSET

Sometimes we are stuck with our parents' fixed (unchanging) mindsets. We had questions and wanted answers, but all we got was, "Because I said so." That didn't answer the question. And so, a lot of times, our parents grew up with fixed mindsets based on the fixed mindsets of their mothers and the fixed mindsets of their mother's mother. So, a mindset can become generational if we allow it to. To keep this from happening, it is important to realize that the way we do things today is not the way things were done in the past. Be willing to grow into a new mindset that aligns with the core values and beliefs of the family you desire to build.

Because dating has changed over the years, I had to develop a growth mindset with my teenage daughter. People thought I was crazy when I encouraged her to not be committed to exclusively dating one boy until she knew what she liked and didn't like in boys. Too often I saw the pattern of a girl meeting a boy, liking him, giving him all her time, attention and whatever else she wanted to give him, all for it to be over in 2 weeks. These are teenage boys with the attention span of a gnat. They don't know what they want at this age and neither did my daughter. The only way to find out is to date different guys to see what qualities she liked and what qualities she didn't like. Hear me clearly. I didn't say have sex or become emotionally attached. I said date. For me, dating is defined as going out on dates, in groups, asking questions for the purpose of getting to know someone better. I told her once she figures out what she likes and doesn't like, then she can consider an exclusive relationship. That didn't happen until she was 17 and I think this way served her well and saved her from getting too emotionally attached until she knew what she wanted. She got to choose who was best for her. This was contrary to how I was raised and what society teaches: women should wait to get chosen. This was a total mindset shift for me, and it worked for my family. My mother would have never encouraged me to do that.

All the mixed messages we get in society can be awfully confusing to young developing minds. **MAJOR KEY: Having a growth mindset and being willing to look at things from a different perspective and not just the perspective in which we were raised is key.** Not being open to changing and growing your mindset can be very dangerous. There are young people today that are homeless, suicidal and depressed because their parents had a fixed mindset about sexuality and gender and refused to accept their children as LGBTQ. Children may feel that they were born this way, while their parents may see it as a choice or an abomination (religious mindset). Being closed minded in this area has caused the breakup and break down of many families. The older a parent is, the more fixed their mindset may be. Be willing to abandon old school ways that exist for no other reason than that is just how it is.

Unfortunately, between society, our families, school, media and the church, there have been many bad seeds that were planted in our minds that need to be uprooted. I am not even going to call them seeds. I'm going to call them weeds because they don't belong in our psyche. They don't belong in our thought life. So we must be willing to pull up the weeds and plant new seeds of growth and change.

START HERE

Let's begin with how we think about ourselves as women. Women are freaking amazing, let's face it. We have resilience and amazing creativity. We are problem solvers and world changers. We thrive in the toughest circumstances. And let's not forget, we give birth! That alone is a feat designed only for a woman. Let's replant seeds that tout the wonderfulness of being an authentic woman who says yes, we do have a voice. Yes, we can stand up for what we believe in. Yes, it's okay to cry. It's okay to have feelings. It's okay to not do it all. It's okay to not be a superwoman. We must stand up for what we believe in and not necessarily what people say we should believe in. If you don't know who you are or what you believe in, find out so you can teach those things to your daughter.

Sometimes people don't take the time to know what they believe, their core values. As I mentioned earlier, my core values and beliefs are based on the five F's - faith, family, fun, friendships and finances. Faith is a very important part of my life. I made sure to teach my children how much God loves them and the importance of having a relationship with Him and serving Him and others in this life. Family is extremely important to me, and I've communicated to my daughter how family is a source of comfort, strength and pride. Family is a safe place where she can feel seen and heard. Life is meant to be enjoyed, so fun is something we value. We are a big gaming family and love games of all kinds. My children have watched me maintain meaningful friendships their entire lives. I taught my daughter to value true friends who encourage and support her, and she can do the same for them. My last core value is finances. I taught my children to be financially resourceful and responsible. I don't want finances to be an obstacle to any opportunity they desire.

How do I apply these values to my everyday life? When my mindset or thoughts want to go in a negative direction or I am getting discouraged about something, I remind myself of my core values. I say, "Hey, I can't do this. But I can lean on my family or my support system of friends to encourage me." When I'm doubting myself, I can turn to my faith and prayer for direction and wisdom instead of beating myself up. Moms, I don't want you to beat yourself up for what you've done or didn't do. That is not the point of this book. There will be no beating ourselves up. What I want you to do is recognize the things in your mind that keep you stuck and keep you doing the same things over and over that you really don't want to do. I want you to recognize those things in your mind that keep you from having open, honest and authentic conversations with your daughter. Is it easy? Heck no. It is difficult. It is difficult to reveal that we make mistakes. It is difficult to reveal that we don't know what we're doing sometimes. It is difficult to reveal how we've handled relationships so poorly. And it's embarrassing sometimes, but that doesn't mean it can't be done. We don't want to live in shame because shame is something that will keep you stuck. And when we are vulnerable and reveal what we are ashamed of, we are set free. The shame is removed because it has been exposed. If you struggle with shame, please read Brene Brown's book, *The Gifts of Imperfection*. It will help you tremendously.

CHAPTER CONCLUSION

I encourage you to really examine your thoughts and develop a growth mindset. Warped mindsets hold you back and may be holding your daughter back. Maybe your daughter has it in her mind that you don't want to hear what she has to say. Work on changing that. Let her know you do want to hear what she has to say.

Your mindset matters. Very little will change if you don't change your mindset. Your ability to do what you need to do and bridge the gaps between you and your daughter begins with a change in how you think. Do you believe teenagers don't listen? They don't care. Change that, because I am here to tell you that they do listen. They do care and they will listen to those who value what they have to say.

Momma, your mindset is the foundation that will determine how you and your daughter connect. This chapter is the first building block for authentic conversations to take place, because if you don't approach your daughter with the right mindset, none of the suggestions I give will matter. Start with believing that as a mom you have tremendous influence and power to shape your daughter's future. And with great power, comes great responsibility. It is your responsibility to have a growth mindset that welcomes new ideas and new ways of doing things.

QUESTIONS

Do you believe you have a growth mindset or fixed mindset? Why?

ACTION

Take the MINDSET QUIZ in the Appendix to find out.

AFFIRMATION

I am ready, open and willing to change the thoughts that do not serve me.

Fixed Mindset Vs. Growth Mindset

Fixed Mindset Is Limiting

- *Talents, abilities, and intelligence is fixed, it's who we are*
- *Avoids challenges*
- *Gives up easily*
- *Avoids new experiences with fear of failure*
- *Looks for people who can reinforce their self-esteem*

Growth Mindset Is Freedom

- *Talents, abilities, and intelligence can be developed through effort and practice*
- *Embraces challenges*
- *Perseveres in the face of failures and setbacks*
- *Looks for people who challenge them to grow*
- *Focuses on the process and learning without worrying about the outcome*

Chapter Six

SEEK TO UNDERSTAND

Dear Mom,

I know you say you want me to talk to you, but when I try you seem upset. Sometimes when I tell you stuff, you just roll your eyes and once you even said I was being disrespectful because I disagreed with you, but I wasn't. I struggle a lot with my self-esteem and just wish you would support me sometimes and sometimes just listen more. I feel like when I get older, our relationship might not be that close because I feel like we argue all the time and we are drawing apart. Please try to understand me and what I am going through.

I love you,
Pharrah, 14

I know we've all heard the saying listen to understand and not to respond. Seeking to understand is a lost art in today's social media world. Everybody who has an opinion makes it known and feels like they must share their opinion about everything, even when it's not asked for. Often, when people are speaking on social media, they are just seeking to respond. They are not really seeking to understand what the person is saying. They are not pausing or taking a beat to say, "Hey, let me examine this person's thoughts or perspective. And even if I don't agree, I can allow this person to express their opinion." Society has gotten so used to just responding and not truly understanding.

TIMES ARE A CHANGING

Listening is a lost art in today's society. Sometimes when I'm trying to explain something like online dating or selfies to my 85-year-old mother, she finds it hard to understand that times have changed. Going out, men courting you, meeting up for a date, asking for your phone number, calling you and leading the whole way is not something we do in the 2020s. The old way of dating is practically dead and has been replaced with virtual dates, wyd texts and dating multiple people. Since the advent of online dating, people from different countries, cities, and states have met and many have found love. It's a new way of doing things. This is very hard for my mother to understand and because she lacks understanding of the changing times, it's hard for her to accept the new way and how I choose to date.

Another example of how things have changed is how we read and take in information. Before, books could only be found in paper form. Now we have audible and video forms. Some people still love paperbacks and hardcovers. They refuse to listen to a book. "That's not reading!" they say, but in the end the same goal is accomplished.

Change is inevitable. When we are responding to our daughters and seeking to understand them, which is what we should be doing, we have to realize that change is necessary and allows us to be open to understanding their world better. We might not understand everything they're talking about, but this is our opportunity to listen and not think about responding.

SILENCE IS NOT GOLDEN

A lot of us were silenced as children. We were silenced at home and told to be quiet at school (raises hand). As we got older, we were silenced by the media, by men, the church and corporate America. When we're taught to be silent, we lose our voice. **MAJOR KEY: Instead of saying, be seen and not heard, we should be saying we see you and we hear you, because that's what kids want to know - that we see them, and we hear them.** Sometimes you don't even have to respond, just acknowledge that you see your daughter.

When I was a teacher, one thing that used to really anger parents is when teachers or the administration did not respond to their calls or requests. I remember when I used to accompany my principal in parent conferences for African American parents. She was very uncomfortable with conflict and confrontation, and especially uncomfortable talking to African American parents, and asked me to sit in the meetings as a mediator. I quickly discovered the problem though. By the time parents secured a meeting with her, they were already angry. Why? Because they weren't heard the other four times they called to get their issue resolved.

How it happened at this particular school was that parents would call the secretary and ask to speak to the principal. The principal would tell the secretary she isn't available or that she would call them back. When that didn't happen, the parents would call again. The principal would tell the secretary to say she wasn't available, or that she would call them back. The parent would call the third time with the same request and get the same answer and no call back. With each of these messages, parents became more and more irate and rightly so. They had a pressing issue that they wanted to discuss with the principal, and they were being ignored. Can any of you relate?

While it didn't start off with anger, people don't really like being ignored. For the parents, not being seen or heard angered them before the conference even began. Not only were they upset about what originally happened, now they were also upset about being ignored. To them, it appears that the principal didn't see them or their problem as important enough to address in a reasonable time frame. Therefore, I sat in on the meetings, because my principal at the time felt like parents always came in angry and she wanted a barrier to assist her in "calming" them down. The same thing can happen with our daughters if we silence them - intentionally or unintentionally. If we put them off, if we always respond when they have something to say, if we put other things before their requests to speak with us, they will think we are not interested in them or what they have to say. And sometimes they will be correct. And sometimes they will be angry.

CULTIVATING COMMUNICATION

To understand how to cultivate authentic communication with your daughter, here are some questions I want you to ask her when she comes to you and says, "Hey Mom, can we talk about something?"

1. Ask yourself if you have the capacity to listen or would another time be better. Let's face it. Some topics need a lot of energy to talk about. As a mom, I know you have a lot going on. At the end of a busy and stressful day may not be a good time to have a serious conversation. If you don't have the capacity to listen, set a date and time to talk and stick to it. Show up ready to listen.

2. Ask your daughter if she is seeking advice, your opinion, or does she just want you to listen. Whatever her answer is, just do that. I know it will be hard. If she says just listen, she may want advice or your opinion later. If she just wants you to listen, when she is done, thank her for sharing. Depending on what she wants to talk about, there may be actions she needs

to take. If so, ask her: What do you plan on doing? Again, just listen. If you feel compelled to give advice or an opinion, ask: Do you mind if I gave you some advice or would you like to hear my thoughts?

3. How would you like me to help you with this? Once she's shared and does want your help, ask how she wants that to look. Don't just barge in and do it your way. It may be just supporting or cheering her on. It may be talking to a teacher or someone who is bullying her. It may be giving her the tools to solve the problem herself. The key here is to ask and only insert yourself as suggested. Once she knows you respect her voice, she will share it more freely.

Now let me put a caution here. If your daughter shares life altering or life-threatening news, TAKE IMMEDIATE ACTION. I want no harm to come to your daughter or another person. Clear? Good!

I saw a technique on social media that I love because I have very vivid facial expressions which sometimes tell how I feel before my mouth does. I see you agreeing. It's a great way for you to be authentic about how you are feeling, along with giving your daughter the freedom to speak candidly. I call this technique pillow talk. Sit side by side with a little space in between the two of you. Then hold up a pillow between your heads so that neither of your faces can be seen. It's almost like sitting in a confessional with a priest with the wall between you and your daughter. This gives my face the freedom to express how I am feeling without my daughter seeing anything that might be interpreted as shock, disappointment, anger, etc. This gives her the freedom to speak authentically. Mom, you still get to release some of the emotion that you are feeling, and your daughter gets to feel safe in expressing herself. This is an amazing way to have a conversation, especially when discussing an intense or sensitive topic. The first time may be awkward, but I think it's a great way for all parties to feel comfortable. Try it and see if it works for you and your daughter.

When YOU want to talk to your daughter about something, ask her: "Is this a good time to talk?" She might be having a bad day or be on her menstrual cycle. She might be emotional about something else that has nothing to do with you. And if she says no, follow up with: When is a better time to talk? Then hold her to that time. Let her know you expect her to honor that time. Moms get shut out many times when they want to talk, simply because they don't ask permission. I know these are new concepts for many of us. You want me to ask my daughter for permission to ask her a question? Yup, I sure do. Think of how much smoother your day would go, if others asked you for permission to share their thoughts instead of just dumping on you regardless of how you are feeling. Exactly.

As a society, we have to get over this notion that children don't have a voice. Let your daughter know that she does have a voice and you are open to hearing it, respectfully. When you allow her to express herself freely, she will share more. If you react in any way that violates her trust, makes her afraid or fearful or makes her feel unworthy or insecure, that may be the last time she shares something with you. And that is not what you want.

IT'S NOT ABOUT YOU

The purpose of this book is to foster communication, understanding and connection, and you cannot do that if you are responding with fear, scare tactics, harsh words or your own personal journey. When your daughter shares something with you, be sure not to make it about you. Telling your story is fine when it's appropriate or requested. But if your daughter is explaining to you that a friendship she valued has ended because of a misunderstanding, this is not the time to insert your personal story and views about failed friendships and how you don't trust women, unless she asks you to do so. Don't make it about you. If your daughter wants to hear your story about how you handled a similar situation, then tell her. But if she doesn't want to hear your story, just be prepared to listen and to understand.

As you go back and remember what it was like for you as a young girl, remember that the things our parents may have deemed unimportant or easy to get over were very serious and important to us. Remember? Losing friendships, being teased, being bullied, not having the right clothes, not having the right hairstyle, not being accepted by our peer group and just figuring out who we are is very important. These are the building blocks of our self-esteem, our identity and self-worth. Most young people have not had enough practice in those areas to just be bold and proud of who they are and what they are. It's a muscle that must be built, cultivated and developed with love and understanding. We build that muscle by learning who we are and becoming confident in our truth. We build that muscle when we have a community of safe trusted adults, who not only support and reinforce what we have to say, but also listen and understand what we have to say. You are a part of that community. I encourage you to ensure you are not the only one that your daughter can talk to. Build a support system of trusted adults who share your values and love for her. These can be sisters, aunts, grandmothers, coaches, friends, pastors and even social media personalities. Use these people as long as you are comfortable with them giving your daughter advice. The litmus test is if they would give the same or similar advice or communicate similar values as you would. These are people that she can go to for another perspective or to discuss situations that you may not have experience with. Build this community for your daughter because it's about her well-being.

My daughter didn't know this, but I enlisted the help of her 3rd grade teacher, Mrs. Kelly, as a part of her support system. When I was going through a situation with my daughter, or I felt she was going through something and didn't want to talk to me about it, I talked to her 3rd grade teacher and asked her to be a sounding board for my daughter. My daughter loved and admired Mrs. Kelly and Mrs. Kelly was not only a professional colleague, but also a trusted friend who genuinely loved her students and my daughter. I trusted any help or advice she might give. She found a way to bring up my concern in a conversation and listen or help as needed. As we know, our children will sometimes listen to everyone but us. Even if that person says the same exact thing we said. I guess it just sounds better coming from someone else. I am not saying run around telling all your friends about your daughter's problems or concerns but do identify other people who will agree to stand in the gap when you can't, or to reinforce what you want your daughter to know, or just provide loving support when needed.

LET HER LEAD THE WAY

I had to learn to do these things and put them into practice because I wanted to understand my daughter better. The girls I have worked with over the years taught me how they wanted to be treated. They shared with me what would help them better navigate the challenges they face daily. Having someone to talk to that they can trust tops the list. Students have all always shared with me how they just wanted to be heard and understood.

I created an award-winning mentorship program for high school girls called Jasira. We would meet every Wednesday over a meal. The meal was the draw, but I think what the girls enjoyed most about the program was the opportunity to be understood, to be listened to, and to be heard. Many topics were discussed, and we listened to each other without judgment. They found out during those times that they were not alone in how they felt. Many times, they would share with me how they just wished their parents understood and were willing to listen to them. If you let her lead the conversation and you simply listen, you will learn a lot.

Now I usually get some flack for this one. But I will take it because I hear girls say this often as well. It's not your responsibility to be your daughter's best friend. It's your responsibility to be her parent. Let me tell you why I say this. While parenting and friendship both have enjoyable aspects that overlap, think about how you behave, what you say and what you share with your closest, bestest friends. Do you WANT to interact with your daughter in that same way? Do you want to share with her how your partner is insensitive to your needs, or tell her the negative thoughts you sometimes have about mommying? I don't think so.

We emotionally dump on our closest friends. Often, (if we have true great friends) we share our most vulnerable and not so proud moments. Our daughters don't need or want that type of relationship with us, nor do we want to know EVERYTHING about them either. Trust me, you don't. She can share with her friends how she really feels about you at times, what she really wanted to say or do to that boy, or how she really hates something you want her to like. She can share these things without judgment. If she shared everything with you and you shared everything with her, the emotional toll would be great. That's one of the reasons we have friends, to help relieve some of our emotional baggage and to support us as needed. I hope you see where I am coming from here. Bonding and sharing experiences with your daughter is amazing and it feels a lot like friendship at times, and that's awesome. But at the end of the day, you are the parent, and she is looking for you to be that. Whew, we've gotten that out of the way. Being a parent is being a leader and leading by example. When you lead by example, you sometimes must go against the grain and make unpopular choices and decisions. Take pride in being her mommy who sometimes connects with her like a friend. It is very important not to confuse those roles.

The more you understand your daughter's thoughts, the better chance you have of influencing positive change in her life. For example, if your daughter has a friend that you don't particularly like, calling that person names or saying "your little friend" or degrading them in any way, probably will not change your daughter's mind. Listening to your daughter and understanding what she likes about that person, or even just what she likes in a friend will give you an opportunity to express your thoughts.

I'll give you an example of something I see often. Let's say your daughter has a friend that is a mean girl. She may really like her one on one or like just being around her for whatever reason. She tells you that at school the friend is very mean to other girls, a bully. Your daughter is struggling with this. So what do you do? What would you say? Pause here to think about it. Most parents would discourage the friendship saying, you shouldn't be friends with her because she's a bad example and a bad influence on you and you may be right. But that is not going to probably stop your daughter from being around her, especially if she considers her a friend.

However, maybe try asking, "Well, what do you like about her when it's just the two of you hanging out? What do you like about her when she's around others at school? What do you dislike about the way she behaves? Is she open to hearing how she is viewed at school and is she ok with how she is viewed? You're trying to understand what draws your daughter to this particular girl. When you find that out, then you can probe deeper into why she wants to befriend this girl. Maybe she wants to help her change her behavior. Maybe she just doesn't want to be bullied by her, so she befriended her. Maybe she is being bullied into being her friend. The point is, you won't know until you ask questions. Your goal is to try to get your child to see the issue or solution for themselves, because when they see for themselves, they are more likely to make a change. It is very important to give your daughters the power and motivation to change behavior on their own, while you are simply listening and helping them to clarify what's important to them.

This empowers your daughter to know who she is, what she desires and how to use her voice to get it. In our entire history, women's voices have been stifled. We must still fight for the right to be heard in some arenas. As mothers, we have to be proactive in changing that narrative. We have to be proactive in showing our girls that they do have a voice, and there is a way to express themselves so they can be heard and understood. This starts in your household. This is how you change the narrative of how women are seen and understood. Your daughter will have many instances where she will be misunderstood by people. But when we take our time to appropriately model how conversations should look, then she will have an example to refer to when it comes to advocating for what she wants.

CHAPTER CONCLUSION

Changing and examining your language is very critical. Do you say things with sarcasm? Do you always joke about it? Or is your tone harsh or critical? These are things that you have to really look at and say, "Hey, I am seeking to respond more than to understand, but I can change this," because how we say things is just as important as what we say. Once we do our mindset work, and then seek to understand, connection will surely come. And that's what we want because when you have connection, your relationship grows and of course your love for one another just continues to grow.

QUESTIONS

What language do you need to change? What do you need to understand better about today's preteen or teen girl?

ACTIONS

Start building a support system for your daughter. Examine your list of trusted friends and relatives and ask them to support you and your daughter on her journey. Share with your daughter that she has a support system that is available to hear, understand and encourage her.

AFFIRMATIONS

My words have power. I will use this power responsibly.

Earn the right to be heard by listening to others. Seek to understand a situation before making judgments about it.

John C. Maxwell

Chapter Seven

BE PROACTIVE

Dear Mama,

I love you so much. I know sometimes I don't act like it, but I do. I want you to help me as I grow up. I want to know about my body and how I am supposed to take care of myself. I hear a lot of things at school that confuse me, but I don't know how to talk about it. You work hard and sometimes you are so tired, so sometimes I don't want to ask you. I wish we could talk to someone or to each other. I need answers and I feel alone. Can you help me? Thank you, mama. I love you.

Maria, 12

As Boy Scouts say, be prepared. Being proactive about how you approach difficult topics will make you better prepared and more confident. You know what these topics are going to be about already because they were the same things you wanted to discuss with your mother. Your daughter may ask you about your relationship with her father, your childhood, her period, her breasts, boys, how babies are made, jealousy, sexual identity or anything. These are things you know will come up, and the best way to be confident in your approach to communicating about them is to be proactive.

When you were a young girl, do you remember all the things you wanted to know or learn about? Sometimes it shocked our parents when we mentioned things like masturbation, pornography or being attracted to the same sex. In this day and time, society provides a lot of opportunities for those things to be discussed openly through media and other avenues. Always remember that you are your child's first and greatest teacher. You demonstrate and model desired behavior daily. You get to dictate what the norms are for your household. But then your child seeks examples of those norms to be true or false as they go out into the world each day. So being proactive on how you will approach common adolescent topics and concerns is key.

STAY READY

Adolescent behavior is fickle. Adolescent behavior is based upon children finding out who they are, where they fit in, and what they're supposed to do in this world. It's a period of immense change and growth - emotionally, physically and mentally. Your daughter really needs you to be a resource and source of information and inspiration. She is going to come to you for affirmation, approval and wisdom. She's going to come to you for justification and support. Be prepared to open the dialogue and know where you stand and what you believe. If you feel like you cannot adequately talk about puberty and adolescence, find out how. This is the information age. Don't be afraid to refresh your memory and read up on it.

There's a saying: Stay ready so you don't have to get ready. And that is pretty much what you're doing when you are being proactive. You know these topics will come up so prepare for them. Prepare to discuss them with factual information that actually teaches your daughter what to do in certain situations. Be very practical in your approach. Teach your daughter what consent is and what it is not. Teach her about good touches and bad touches. Show her how to know and explore her own body and how different body parts function. She is going to seek out the information anyway. So don't be appalled that she wants to know. You did too. Share your stories of difficulty in dealing with self-identity or self-esteem. Be careful not to dump, and if you have unhealed trauma, please see a therapist. Your daughter is not your therapist.

From reading the earlier chapters, you may have discovered that you are really not equipped to have these conversations because some of these topics may trigger unpleasant experiences. I want you to get help. I want you to go to a therapist, pastor, priest or a trusted counselor to work out your issues because you don't want to bring your issues, biases, or trauma into your daughter's life. I've seen this a lot in the families I work with. **MAJOR KEY: Trauma is usually generational, until someone stops it. Be the one, momma.** The only way you can effectively heal yourself is by going to a professional to get help. And that is perfectly fine. I'm so happy that we are finally normalizing mental health. Also, don't be afraid to do your research or take a class on topics you need to understand better.

JUST THE FACTS

Don't be afraid to speak to your child's needs. I know when I was a teenager, and probably some of you have experienced this as well, the main message parents gave to girls was don't be fast and don't get pregnant. They really didn't want to talk about or explain the ins and outs of a dating relationship, how to set boundaries with young boys, or how to make sure your standards are respected. They didn't really discuss what was a good touch and what was a bad touch. They didn't discuss how to assert yourself or how to get out of difficult situations you find yourself in. They just didn't want you to come home pregnant. I think mainly because they didn't want to be embarrassed or pegged as a bad mom. Explaining sex, procreation, reproduction and puberty is so important because there is much misinformation in the streets.

Once a student told me that she thought she was pregnant. (I used to be a sexual health educator.) When I spoke to her about it further, she had engaged in oral sex with a young man, and then she didn't have her period the next month. One of her friends told her that because she missed her period, she might be pregnant. She knew that she did not have intercourse with this young boy, but her friend told her that it didn't matter whether she had intercourse or not. The friend explained, when you have oral sex, sperm can go down your throat into your womb and impregnate you. And this young girl was terrified that she was pregnant. I informed her of the facts of oral sex and intercourse and explained how conception occurs. I let her know where to get a discreet pregnancy test if she wanted to alleviate her fears. Having oral sex does not impregnate you and teaching your daughter these facts without using scare tactics is very helpful. Sometimes parents just try to scare the behavior out of children and that just never works. Factual information is needed in this world of misinformation. This is only one of many stories I could share about misinformation.

Have you ever been to a party or event and there was a boy or girl who was pressuring you to do something you really didn't want to do? (I see your hand.) Well, let's prepare to talk to our daughters about that. Usually, parents don't find out about these situations until after the fact. But what if you prepared for this conversation in advance. It will happen to 90% of girls. Here's an example of what to say.

"Hey daughter, if you're at a party and a boy tries to pressure you to do something you don't want to do, like take a drink, smoke something or go to a separate room with him, do you know how to negotiate out of that safely?"

If she says no, give her these tips:

- Say NO firmly if you don't want to do it.
- Keep repeating NO until he gets the message.
- If he doesn't get the message, ask for help from anyone who is around. Don't be afraid because your life/health could be at stake.
- Yell NO if you have to. Again, be firm.
- Tell him, if he doesn't stop, you will call for help - the police, your parents, etc.
- Feel free to call me (mom) at any point in this exchange. I will come get you no questions asked. Then keep your word, mom.

As a sexual health educator, I realized that these life skills just aren't taught often enough. Not teaching them can lead to trauma, abuse or even death. In my classes, we would role play all kinds of situations and the girls would be surprised that they could have a plan. Doing a little research on these things will definitely help you become a better communicator and resource to your daughter. She will come to you because she knows you have answers, and you won't freak out.

I mentioned this before, but it bears repeating. Please don't tell horror stories or lies that evoke fear in your daughter, hoping it will deter her behavior. All it will do is evoke fear and anxiety and that doesn't work in building connection. Most have heard the lie that masturbation will make you blind. That statement may make you laugh, but it's not funny because it's a lie. If it wasn't, everyone would be blind. This is not a plug for masturbation. But why would anyone say or think that when masturbation is a natural and normal part of growing up and should be communicated as such.

Be prepared for these hard topics and provide your daughter with truth and facts. She will appreciate your honesty and know she can trust you to tell her the truth, whether you agree with what she is doing or not. Know your values and be ready to communicate them in a loving way. We want to teach our daughters how to think, not what to think.

I used to think having an orgasm was a bad thing because that's what I was taught. I was taught that feeling sexy or knowing what your body looks like was bad. There's a lot of shame and bad feelings around masturbation and understanding how your body works and what arouses us. This should not be a scary subject. It is a natural part of life. The Creator gave us those feelings. Yes, we have to use them responsibly, but we have them, and they cannot be wished away. I think you can totally honor your faith and be in tune with and understand your body. I believe that's God's intention.

Maybe your hope for your daughter is to one day meet and marry a wonderful person. However, (as we women can testify) I think a lot of confusion comes in marriage when women don't know what they want. Then they say men don't know how to please or satisfy them. But they don't even know how they like to be satisfied. All they do know is that whatever he's doing is not satisfying them. They have not done enough self-exploration, or don't have enough understanding of their body to know what satisfies them at all. So that's another reason why having the correct information, purchasing a book on adolescence or puberty, or going through a puberty course with your child is helpful because it gives you tools to use in speaking factually about those things.

PRACTICE EVENTUALLY MAKES PERFECT

Talking to my own daughter and son about these things was extremely awkward. I noticed things, but lots of times didn't say anything. I missed some naturally teachable opportunities to have important conversations, but I didn't quite know how. I was unprepared and embarrassed to discuss these things. So I am right there with you momma. I can relate. Listen, some conversations are just going to be awkward and we have to be proactive in preparing for that.

I used to practice in the mirror talking to my daughter about things that I really didn't want to have conversations about, so I could figure out what I would like to say before the topic ever came up. I wanted to make sure I could control my emotions. I'd ask my reflection things like, "What do you think about sex? Are you interested in girls?" Then I practiced what I was going to say if she said yes, or what I was going to say if she said I don't want to follow the faith you follow. I had to prepare myself for those things because our children are individuals. They're not mini me's. They're not us. So preparing for these difficult conversations in advance will help you navigate them better.

Practicing these conversations and unlocking the communication blocks you have is a good way to increase understanding and build connection. When you practice these conversations, you come to your daughter from a place of confidence and love, because you have taken the time to prepare for what may come and educated yourself on the things you need to know to give your daughter confidence. Many parents do not take the time to prepare. They just leave it to chance.

I've heard so many horror stories about how girls/women found out about their periods. That's not how it should be. Now, I assume that the mother was uncomfortable with having that conversation. But if she would have practiced telling her daughter about her menstrual cycle, she would have been more comfortable. We know your daughter is going to get a period unless there's a medical reason why she can't. So why not prepare for that in advance by telling her what happens, how to use certain products, how to take care of her body, how to take care of her hygiene, and how to avoid being embarrassed at school. Talk to her about these things.

You know your daughter is going to be interested in boys, or girls maybe. Prepare yourself for those conversations by learning how to give practical and factual advice that empowers her to make good decisions and feel secure in who she is. The more proactive you are, the better connection you will make and there is a better chance that your daughter will continue coming to you for help, advice and support. When you prepare for these conversations, they get easier to have. You don't have to be afraid to have them because doing so will also allow you to be more vulnerable and vulnerability builds connection.

CHAPTER CONCLUSION

Stick to the facts and be authentic in your conversations. If you don't know something, tell your daughter you don't know. You can find out together. But tell her you'll find out and we'll discuss it together at this day and time. If you don't know something, it's also okay to enlist the help of a gynecologist, medical professional or therapist. Make sure this is ok with your daughter because you want her to buy in. You don't want to <u>make</u> your daughter see a therapist, psychologist or a gynecologist. One reason is she may not want to share with that person, and it may seem like you don't want to deal with it. Another reason is you can waste a lot of money having your daughter in a therapist's or gynecologist's office just staring at each other. I've seen it happen.

There are good reasons to enlist the help of a professional. If you have severe trauma around these issues, if your daughter has special needs or her own trauma around these issues, professionals can help you bridge the communication gap and give you the language you need. We know these conversations are coming, so be proactive.

QUESTION

What's one topic you need to read up on or research so you can be prepared for that conversation?

ACTIONS

Review factual information about puberty and adolescence. Write down your core values so you can share them with your daughter. If necessary, make an appointment for the two of you to speak to a gynecologist or other health professional.

AFFIRMATIONS

I will prepare to learn what I don't know. I will choose facts over scary stories.

Notes

Write down questions you have or topics you still want to learn more about. Research them and find answers so you can be prepared to talk about them when the time comes.

Chapter Eight

UNLOCKING YOUR COMMUNICATION BLOCKS

Dear Mommy,

This is a hard letter to write. I have been through so much during my teen years that still haunt me as an adult. You know about some of it, but there's a lot you don't know about. I wanted you to love me just as I am instead of yelling, hitting or cussing at me. Now, I can see that I didn't deserve that. But it was hard to believe that I was a good person as a teenager.

Being the only girl, you seemed to put all the blame on me, while giving my brothers a pass. I didn't understand this. I know it's hard to raise kids, but I felt like you were always angry with me, and I didn't know why. I was glad I had a mentor to talk to and process some of my feelings because if not, I may not be here. I tried to harm myself several times because

I didn't feel worthy or loved. I just wished you could have loved me for me, talked to me, listened to me, understood me.

There are so many feelings going through my mind right now, but I'll just sum it up here. I believed you loved me in the way you knew how. Unfortunately, it didn't feel like love. I know you tried to get help with your anger, but I still seemed to be the target of your rage. I tried very hard to be the daughter you wanted and still don't know if I am. But I have to be ok with that. I have my own children and don't want to see them go through what I did, so I have to forgive you and carry on. I forgive you ma, and I love you.

Carrie, 37

Everything you've read so far leads you to this chapter of practical application. You probably won't unlock your communication blocks, until you process the information in the first seven chapters. One thing I've found in my interactions with mothers and daughters is that many times mothers have some communication blocks. These are behaviors that hinder effective communication. Although well meaning, some things we say and do as moms, shut down communication instead of encouraging it. This is understandable because if you've never been taught or never witnessed effective communication, how would you know how to do it. In this chapter I want to talk about those communication blocks and how to overcome them.

COMMUNICATION BLOCKS

There are 6 ways that we block effective communication with our daughters.

1. **Asking why questions.** On the surface this may not seem like a communication block. After all, what's wrong with asking why? Usually nothing. But when mothers ask why to daughters and depending on how you say it, it can be seen as judgment. For example, why do you want to go to that party? Usually the tone is disapproving. Also, you will probably not get an answer that tells you what you really want to know. Try asking who, what or how instead of why. For example: Using the party question from above - Who's going to be at the party? How long will you be there? What kind of party is it? Not only do these questions give you more specific information, but they also tend to communicate curiosity instead of judgment.

2. **Giving quick reassurance.** When your daughter comes to talk to you, giving quick reassurance doesn't give you or her time to process the information. Quick reassurance sounds like, "Oh, don't worry." "You'll get through it." "It's no big deal." "You'll get over it." Again, these phrases sound reassuring, and they can be once you have taken the time to listen, understand and process. But giving QUICK reassurances is like saying, "I don't want to hear more." Take time to listen, understand and

process the information first, and then suggest a positive outcome. For example, saying something like, "I hear and understand your concern. I believe if you let your friend know that chewing with her mouth open at lunch bothers you, the two of you can work it out." This sounds better than just saying, "You'll work it out." Do you see the difference?

3. **Giving unsolicited advice**. I know. I know. You're the mom. That's what you do. Give your advice and opinion. How's that working for you? In a previous chapter, remember when I suggested that you ask your daughter if she wants you to listen, advise or just support? Sometimes your daughter is not seeking your advice, she is simply wanting your ear or your support. Most of the time when you tell her what you think she should do, it's coming from an adult perspective, not a teen age one. Instead of saying "I think the best thing for you to do is…" You want to empower her to come up with a solution by asking power questions. (That's the next section.)

4. **Patronizing** - Patronizing is when someone communicates with an air of superiority or an attitude of better than. Saying things like, "Sure, you do." "Yes, dear, very interesting." "Oh, you poor thing, I know exactly how you feel." "This is far too complicated for you to understand." Patronizing is a communication block for the obvious reason. It makes your daughter feel like what she said is not really important, or maybe even stupid. You don't know how she feels, so communicating that you do sends a message that you don't really care how she feels

about the subject. Patronizing can also sound like criticism. "You're not wearing that, are you?" These kinds of statements tell your daughter that you know best, so there's no need for her input.

5. **Preaching** - Preaching is going on and on about the ins and outs, dos and don'ts of said topic. We've all probably been the recipient of our mother's preaching about boys, sex or something we wore. Saying "You shouldn't do this or You shouldn't do that" sounds like it's coming from a place of judgment and communicates a holier than thou attitude. Preaching is ineffective for 2 main reasons. One, after the first 5 minutes, your daughter is no longer listening. Did you listen to your parents when they droned on and on about something. Two, it involves more talking than listening. Once your daughter sees that you are not open to listening, just giving your opinion, communication is blocked.

6. **Interrupting** - There is not much explanation needed for this one. Jumping in and assuming you know what your daughter is going to say is not only ineffective communication, but also rude. Think about how you feel when someone interrupts you when you are talking. It doesn't feel good to you and it will not feel good to your daughter. Allowing her to have her say makes her feel heard, seen and respected. Resist the urge to interrupt by using active listening techniques.

LISTENING TECHNIQUES

As you can see mom, this is not as easy as you may have thought, but with consistent practice, you can be an effective communicator. There are 4 listening techniques that you can employ to help you achieve your goal. If you recognize that you use some of the communication blocks listed above, effective listening techniques will help you begin to unblock the flow of communication.

1. **Active listening** - Active listening is being fully present in the moment and giving full attention to the person that is talking. When you actively listen, there are no distractions. Go to a place that is quiet. Put away your phone, turn off the television and stop whatever you're doing. Make sure your body language is open and inviting. No folded arms, crossed legs, crossed eyes, nothing crossed. Shoulders and hands are relaxed and make eye contact. I know making eye contact can make some people uncomfortable, but with practice it will get easier and become the norm. Lean in with your body and nod your head occasionally to acknowledge what your daughter is saying. Pay attention to the question or response and be fully engaged. Active listening is an opportunity for you to hear key words or phrases that you can explain or ask about later.

2. **Reflective listening** - Reflective listening allows you to understand your daughter better by paraphrasing what she is saying. This has three main purposes: to let her know you are listening, to make sure you have clarity about what she is saying, and to help her reflect on her own words. When paraphrasing you might say, "Are you saying…" or "So you feel…when… You are simply giving back to her what she is saying. Be careful not to paraphrase more than twice in a conversation, because it will sound like you're mimicking her instead of listening. Reflective listening also helps your daughter recognize what she's saying and whether or not what she's saying is clear. For example, if you paraphrase what your daughter said and she says, "No, that is not what I meant to say," she has an opportunity to clarify her thoughts. When you speak her thoughts aloud, it helps her hear how it sounds as well. Our teenage daughters don't always know how to express themselves clearly, so reflective listening provides instant feedback and clarification if necessary. Reflective listening also allows your daughter to take ownership for what she is saying. For example, saying "You were upset when…", or "You were feeling frustrated when…," or "You believe that…" These phrases allow your daughter to reflect on what she said. She may not realize that she was upset, frustrated or believed something until it is paraphrased for her. She may discover that wasn't her feeling

after all, or she can take responsibility for her feelings. Reflective listening lets your daughter know that these are her words, not yours. Again, be careful not to overuse reflective listening. Also, pay attention to your daughter's body language and you can make mental notes about what topics make her excited, nervous, anxious or sad.

3. **Silence** - Many people are uncomfortable when there is silence. When having important conversations with your daughter, silence is a very effective tool. Silence is an effective technique because it allows both parties to pause and process what they are thinking and what they are saying. Mom, it's ok to pause and be silent when you are communicating with your daughter. Let her know you are pausing to think and to process. When you allow for silence, you give space for your daughter to continue talking and possibly come up with a solution herself because you left space for her to do so. Usually when there is silence, your daughter is going to try to fill that void, and in doing so she will think more about the problem and dig deeper for a solution. Many times, teens don't get the space to talk, think, pause and reflect. Silence gives them that space and it gives you that space. Silence can sometimes be more powerful than your words.

4. **Empathetic Listening** - Empathetic listening means tuning in to how your daughter feels and identifying what

state she is in. Empathetic listening is an acknowledgment of the emotional state of your daughter. For example, if your daughter comes to you and says, "Mom, I had a bad day at school today." The normal response would be, "What happened?" The empathetic response would be, "I see that you are upset, do you want to talk about it?" The latter response showed that you tuned in to how she was <u>feeling,</u> not what happened.

Sympathy and empathy are often confused. Sympathy is feeling FOR someone. Empathy is feeling AS someone. Empathy is not saying I know how I would feel in that situation. It is being able to put yourself aside completely and understanding how someone else feels without judging it. This is important because you don't want to respond based on your own thoughts and experiences. This is about your daughter's thoughts and experiences. Empathetic listening is saying, how would I feel if I were them, not how would I feel if it were me? Do you see the difference? Recognizing the difference between sympathy and empathy can be tricky, but again with practice, you can do it. It's hard to keep our emotions out of sensitive issues, especially as it pertains to our children. But showing empathy is one of the most important ways to let your daughter know that she is understood. People want to be heard and understood from their lens and perspective. Empathetic listening allows you to do that.

MAJOR KEY: When your daughter opens up to you, it's a gift. She is being vulnerable and that can be very scary for her. Validate her perspective and views even if you don't agree with them. Practicing and using these listening techniques, not only with your daughter, but with others as well, will go a long way into making it a natural part of how you communicate.

THE POWER OF QUESTIONS

Questions are powerful, and the right questions can guide us in helping our daughters engage in authentic conversations and consider solutions. Questions naturally tell our brain to find an answer. The reticular activating system is like a search engine in our subconscious brain. When we ask a question, our brain begins looking for answers. That's why the questions we ask are very important because they send a signal to our brain to dig deep into our subconscious mind for possible solutions and answers.

Below is a list of the type of power questions you can ask your daughter. These types of questions elicit specific answers and unlock the flow of communication.

1. **What If Questions:** What if questions increase creativity. What if questions are sometimes used negatively, but they can also be used positively. What if questions allow your daughter to come up with good solutions, not only in the present moment, but also when you

are not around. What if questions are basically saying, what is the possibility, and that's powerful for your daughter to know she has options and that there can be more than one solution to a problem.

Examples

"What if you asked the teacher if you could retake the quiz instead of stressing about passing the class?"

"What if I woke you up a half an hour earlier? Would that help you be on time for school?"

"What if Sarah (the "it" girl) is just as worried as you are about her looks?"

2. **Reframing Questions**: Reframing questions presents the question in another way. When you reframe a question, you are asking for the same information, just in a different way. Here are some questions you can use with your daughter to help gain clarity, dig a little deeper, and strengthen communication. Reframing questions are especially effective because they eliminate the yes/no response and require more thoughtful responses.

Examples

Instead of saying why did you do that. Say, "What can you learn from this?"

Instead of saying do you think that was a good idea. Say, "Can you tell me why you thought that was a good idea?"

Instead of saying, "Why did you lie to me?" Say, "Why is it important to tell the truth?"

Can you see how reframing questions help your daughter shift her perspective and eliminate the yes, no responses?

3. **Focusing Questions**: Focusing questions helps your daughter organize the hodgepodge of thoughts that are going on in her head. When we are having discussions, not only are we verbally talking, but there are usually entire dialogs going on in our minds. Focusing questions shut out some of the internal noise and allows your daughter to just focus on one thing at a time.

   Examples:

   "What is the first thing you need to do?" - This helps her just focus on the first thing.

"What would you do in that situation? - Help her look at options and train her mind to focus on the outcome that she wants rather than being stuck thinking about the problem.

When your daughter says, "This isn't possible." or "I can't do it!" Say, "What would happen if you did ...?" This is helping her to think outside of her limitations and create new possibilities.

4. **Reflective Questions** - This type of question helps her reflect on her process and gives her time to pause and think. Reflective questions help bring greater understanding to a situation.

Examples

"How do you feel about...?" "What do you think about...?"

"How do you know that?" - These questions help her know and figure out what she believes.

Example

If your daughter says, "She doesn't like me." Say, "How do you know that? Does this happen 100% of the time? What evidence do you have?" This question helps you know what's actually going on in a situation and allows your daughter to reflect on the facts of the situation.

Sometimes we get stuck on one train of thought or one limiting belief. Asking reflective questions help you move into a place of analyzing that belief and challenging its truth.

TYPES OF QUESTIONS TO AVOID

Leading Questions - These types of questions attempt to make your daughter feel guilty by leading her toward a certain answer and inserting your own opinion. Leading questions imply something that may or may not be true.

Examples

"Don't you want to make mommy happy?"

"Don't you want to be a good Christian girl?" "Don't you want the other girls to like you?"

Remember it's not about you, it's about them. Leading questions are manipulative and should be avoided at all cost.

Closed Questions - Avoid questions that can be answered with yes or no. These are known as closed questions.

If your daughter has the opportunity to exit out of the conversation quickly, most likely she will. Having these conversations are too important, so don't give her that opportunity.

CHAPTER CONCLUSION

Teens will quickly say, "I don't know" even when they know. Your daughter may know the answer to what you are asking her but may have difficulty articulating it. You can help with that by teaching her how to communicate effectively using the strategies discussed in this chapter. You will not only give her tools to be effective with you, but also with others. And she will have the tools to communicate with her future daughter.

Mom, this may be new information to you. You may be wondering how you will transition from what you've been doing to these new strategies. Like Nike says, just do it. Let your daughter know that you realize you need to improve your communication, and you have been reading up on how to do so. You will be trying some new techniques that will help her feel understood, seen and heard. Unlocking your communication blocks, applying effective listening techniques and asking power questions are the keys to changing a closed conversation to an open one.

QUESTIONS

Which one of the communication blocks do you identify with most? Which listening technique are you going to try to unlock your communication blocks?

ACTION

Think of one conversation you want to have with your daughter. Practice the conversation in the mirror using the listening technique you named above and a few of the power questions.

AFFIRMATION

I have the skills to have authentic conversations with my daughter.

Chapter Nine

YOU HAVE THE POWER

Dear Mom,

I appreciate you. I saw your hard work and how you took care of all of us so well. I know you found it hard to be vulnerable because I rarely saw any signs of weakness in you. I am strong because of you. But you never talked about or shared any of your struggles with us. I thought you were perfect. As an adult, I have plenty of struggles and don't always know how to deal with them. I don't always want to be strong. Sometimes I don't tell you about my problems because I feel like you will think I am weak. I wished we would have talked more about real life stuff because it would have helped me deal with some issues I now go through. I needed to be vulnerable around you and I felt like I couldn't. I would have loved to learn how to communicate better because now I'm pretty closed off. I know you did your best and I love you.

Sharise, 33

I want to begin this chapter by first saying, congratulations for recognizing that you are your child's first and greatest teacher. Mommying is a tough job. I just really want to encourage you to continue to build those bonds and connections with your daughter because it's worth it.

One of my goals is to reverse the negative stereotypes that women face about their bodies, identity and self-worth. This will come from surrounding ourselves with women who love themselves unapologetically, love others, and who know how to support and communicate with other women. Fear is a liar. A lot of times we live our lives full of fear - the fear of rejection, not being accepted, not belonging, the fear of what people will think. That's just not a great way to live. Fear is false evidence appearing real. Fear is only fear, because you don't know the unknown. But with the tools that I've given you in this book, I hope I've alleviated a lot of your fear about having these conversations with your daughter.

DO IT AFRAID

Even if you've messed up in the past, overreacted to something that your daughter has told you, responded inappropriately, or you sought to respond instead of understand, there is always hope. We can always do something differently. We can always change. In fact, it's a great lesson when you've made a mistake and take steps to correct it. It's a great lesson for your daughter to see because she will make mistakes and it lets her know that mistakes are ok. With new knowledge, we do new things. With new mindsets, we encourage growth, and that's exactly the stance that we want our daughters to take in life.

I wrote this book afraid. I don't know how people would respond to me encouraging them to speak confidently, frankly and authentically with their daughters. I'm not the perfect mother, so I wondered what people would say. Would they expect me to be a perfect mother? Would they expect that my daughter and I had amazing and authentic conversations all the time? Well, we don't. I believe there is always room for improvement, and we continue to work on our communication now that she is an adult and there are new areas to tackle. One thing is for certain, I will always be her mother and I will always want the very best for her just like you want the very best for your daughter.

Talking to mothers is such a privilege, but also a slippery slope because we are all out here just trying to do our very best. I was nervous about telling mothers what to do. And even though I'm coming from the stance of working with 1000s of girls in various settings and being a confidant and mentor to most of them, writing about this topic was still scary. So, I am challenging you to tackle the teen years afraid, just like I did. We will constantly learn, grow and change. Some days will be hard. You will struggle, yell, be impatient and overreact. But now you have the power to self-correct through self-awareness, authenticity, new information and love.

This book is 20 plus years in the making of saying I'm going to write a book. I was not focused. I didn't have the knowledge that I now have to do what I should have done, but all was done in the right timing. Timing is important. Moms, walk in your power and boss up, because the cost of not building a connection with your teenage daughter is greater than the cost of doing it. You don't have to operate in fear. Because again, fear is a liar. Push through the fear with your faith. And all you need is a little mustard seed of faith to have these conversations. If you're trying some of these things, and they're not working as you would have hoped, keep trying. If your efforts still don't work, try another strategy. Each daughter is unique, and you must learn what works for your individual child. What you did with one daughter may be different than what you have to do with another daughter. Be open to that. Realize that trust and authenticity take time to build.

GIVE YOURSELF GRACE

I had to give myself grace for mistakes that I made when my daughter was a teenager. I've made many mistakes, but I think this is one that I truly regret and still think of today. When my daughter was in eighth grade, I allowed her to go over to a friend's house to spend the night and something happened that night that neither she nor I wanted to happen. She did not tell me about it, but here's how I found out.

One day I was cleaning her room and I saw her unlocked diary on her bed. I did waver and considered whether I should read it or not. But I read it. There was something in her diary that I did not want to hear, and now I was faced with what to do with this information. I had to confront it because it involved her safety and I put that in the hands of another mother, who didn't ensure my daughter was safe. The other mother gave her permission to do something without asking me, and so I had to confront that mother. I believe that but for that mother's negligence, this probably wouldn't have happened. Therefore, I had to let my daughter know that I had read her diary and I would be talking to her friend's mother. I sat down and talked to her and told her I was disappointed in her and I took it personally. (Bad momma) I told yall I didn't have this all figured out. Where was this book when I needed it?

The look on her face made me regret everything. She was in tears. She was horrified and embarrassed, and I will say that I certainly handled the situation the wrong way, because I came to her in judgment, not considering her privacy, feelings and confusion about the whole situation. I was also crying, and I was very emotional about the whole situation because I felt it was something she was not mature enough to handle at that point, and also because I knew I had hurt her. While I did hold her and comfort her, I also chastised her and broke her trust. A trust that took years to rebuild.

This was one of my big mistakes in raising my daughter - reacting instead of responding. After that incident, I realized I had the power to change. I began working to rebuild her trust because

I will never give up on helping her to become the most confident, secure, empowered, loving, kind person that I know she is. So, even as an adult I continually speak life to her and let her know that I'm available to support her in any way I can. If I can do it, so can you. If you made mistakes, forgive yourself, give yourself grace and keep going.

IT GETS EASIER

You do have the power to build a beautiful connection with your daughter, and it gets easier the more you do it. The more you talk, the more you provide a safe space, the more you give yourself grace and accept that you will make mistakes, the easier it becomes. Sometimes you will have to do things by trial and error to see if it works for your daughter, and if not revamp the plan. We have all had instances where we thought something was extremely hard, like writing this book, for example, or learning to drive a car or resolving a conflict with a friend. We knew it was going to be challenging, but when we actually did it, it wasn't as bad as we thought. That's how I want you to look at this process.

I remember one time I had to tell a good friend a hard truth and lesson and I really didn't want to tell her because, of course, I feared that it would destroy our friendship. But I mustered up the courage and I had the conversation with her about a behavior she was exhibiting that was not flattering or healthy. I approached her with love, support and understanding. She was grateful. I provided her with an opportunity to share with me some shame she had encountered in her life. That shame caused her to behave in a way where she overcompensated in relationships with others. Turns out that she wasn't proud of the way she was acting, but also, she didn't know how to deal with the shame. So, she had an opportunity to release that shame and become really vulnerable with me, and then eventually sought out help to change her behavior. So, while I was fearful of the conversation in the beginning, I realized that having the conversation not only helped us grow closer and stronger in our relationship, but it also gave her the courage and space to seek help and become a better, more secure and confident woman.

You see how I handled that with my friend? Well, that's how I should have handled the diary situation with my daughter. **MAJOR KEY: When parents ask me what they should do or say to their daughter when they want to discuss a sensitive topic, I tell them to talk to her in the manner that you would talk to a best friend.** Notice I didn't say be her best friend. We talk to our friends with much more grace and understanding. We usually don't yell at them or approach them in a negative way. Why? Because we want to preserve the friendship. So just like in the example above, we take a beat and think about what we are going to say. We approach the situation seeking to understand and hear their point of view, because our goal is to continue the friendship. The same attitude and posture should be applied to conversations with our daughters. If you wouldn't roll your eyes at our friend, don't roll your eyes at your daughter. If you wouldn't interrupt your friend, don't interrupt your daughter. If you give your friend grace for her mistakes, give your daughter grace as well. When I have something I want to talk to my children about that's a bit sensitive, I ask myself, how would I approach this with Latrayer, my best friend.

If fear of having certain conversations is still gripping you, let me offer one more piece of advice that may help. Think of the worst case scenario. This is the absolute worst thing that can happen if you confront your daughter about an issue, or the worst thing that your daughter may come to talk to you about. Go ahead. Get that thing in your mind. Is it sex, pregnancy, lesbianism, cutting, her cursing you out? What is the worst thing that could happen? I want you to play out the conversation in your head - the emotions, the yelling and screaming, the slap, the running away. Whatever it is, think about it. Now, I want you to ask yourself, if you can recover from that conversation? If the worst thing happened, could you and your daughter find a way to recover? Could you go to therapy or talk it out later when things are calmer? Could you get her a mentor or get yourself some help to deal with your trauma? Could you teach her about responsible sexual activity or find a support group to help you both? Could you recover and figure out a solution? If the answer is yes, then you have just tackled the worst-case scenario and your fears should dissipate. We fear the unknown. Knowing how you will handle a difficult situation if it arises helps to alleviate some of the fears and get back your power. Although we may not really know how we would handle the worst case scenario if it actually occurs, we can have a plan. That's what fire drills are all about, having a plan in case of a fire. When the fire comes, we will still be afraid, but we know we have a plan and intend on following it. You can do the same, momma.

CHAPTER CONCLUSION

Things do get easier as you do them. I hope this will be the beginning of many years of great conversations with your daughter that will strengthen your bond and communication and most importantly, just strengthen your understanding and love for one another. If you want something that you never had, you have to do something that you've never done. You got this momma!

If your daughter is not a teen or pre-teen you can still begin to have these conversations and use these tips because you'll be setting the stage for when they get to be teenagers, before they become aliens. The earlier the better, depending on your daughter's maturity level. You can begin to build trust and a safe space for your daughter as soon as she begins talking. After all, she already trusts you. That trust just wanes over time because moms have reacted in ways where daughters feel unsafe. So, you can use the strategies in this book with younger girls as well.

We must change this narrative for the next generation. We have to allow our daughters to feel, think, speak and be heard. It is so critical. We've done harder things in our life, and this is something that will yield amazing benefits in the end. Are you up for the challenge? I believe you are because you have the power.

QUESTIONS

What is your biggest fear or concern in communicating with your daughter? What is the worst case scenario?

ACTION

Make a list of three to five things that scared you at first, but then you learned how to do them.

AFFIRMATION

I will give myself grace and be patient with the process.

EPILOGUE

As a mother, my job is to take care of the possible and trust God with the impossible.

Ruth Bell Graham

You've reached the end of this book, but not the end of your journey into greatness. You now have the self-awareness, information and strategies to communicate authentically and improve connection with your teenage daughter. I am so proud of you. I am proud of your courage. I am proud that you want to understand your daughter better. I am proud that you're taking the charge to change the narrative about how young girls are seen and heard. This is so important because girls are crying out for our help as you can see in the letters that I've shared with you. These are real girls, and their letters represent what your daughters are going through. You have the permission, the power, the mindset and the opportunity to have the healthy and whole relationship you both always wanted. I salute you!

I got the courage to write this book because I knew mothers needed to hear what I know and what I have been experiencing for the last 32 years as a mentor, teacher and coach. I knew mothers needed to hear what their daughters were communicating to me about how they want to be understood, how they want to be heard, and how they want to be respected and trusted. We must communicate and connect with our daughters in order for them to grow up to be better than we were. We want them to be safe and secure. We want them to be confident and have the power to create the life they desire. Effective communication is a great way to ensure this happens.

Action is required. I hope you answered each question, took each action step and are continuing to affirm and encourage yourself. Communicating with your daughter about tough topics is not only going to improve your relationship with her, but it will also give her the tools and confidence that she needs to one day model great communication for her daughter. Look at you creating a new narrative of healthy, whole communication for generations to come. We don't have to live in the past or do things the way our parents did them. We know for a fact that some of the things that our parents did were wrong. And we don't need to repeat that cycle. Raising a confident daughter will yield a lifetime of wonderful benefits. It takes courage and a willingness to learn, and you have both.

The following is a summary of the main concepts that have been discussed in this book.

EPILOGUE

Chapter One - You Were Made for This - You are thoroughly equipped to have tough conversations with your daughter because you've been there.

Chapter Two - What's Really Going On? - Know what's going on in society, your daughter's generation, on social media and in your daughter's life because things have changed. Being aware of what she deals with daily, will help you understand and connect with her better.

Chapter Three - What's Your Story? - Being self-aware about your own story, how you were raised, and your triggers are key to connecting with your daughter. Work on healing these sensitive areas so that you can give your best self to your daughter.

Chapter Four - Unlearning - There are certain beliefs that were taught to us by our parents, relatives, church family, teachers, peers and the internet/social media that we must unlearn because those thoughts don't support who we want to be and how we want to show up for our daughters.

Chapter Five - Mindset Matters - Recognize your communication blocks and be ready to shift your mindset from a fixed mindset to a growth mindset. One where you are open to understanding and adopting new ideas for the benefit of your daughter.

Chapter Six - Seek to Understand - Our daughters have a voice, and they want to be heard. Let her know that you not only see her, but you are willing to hear her also.

Chapter Seven - Be Proactive - You know what conversations are coming as your pre-teen/teenage daughter matures. Be ready to learn about what you don't know and face those topics with factual information and support.

Chapter Eight - Unlocking Your Communication Blocks - Understanding your communication blocks will help you unlock authentic conversations. Knowing how to listen and use power questions will help you build genuine connection with your daughter.

Chapter Nine - You Have the Power - You can build a stronger bond and authentic connection with your daughter because you have a desire to do so. That desire gives you the power to be bold and fearless so you can help your daughter do the same.

Finally, I want you to celebrate who you are. I want you to celebrate what you're going to do, and I want you to celebrate you and your daughter often. I want you to pick days of the week and times to celebrate and just have fun. Celebrate what you've done as far as communication and unifying your relationship to be one of mutual respect, authenticity and love. That is what we all want.

I know when your child was little, they were the apple of their eye. You provided them with every need. You tried to make life so that they didn't want for anything. They showed great need for you and it's great to feel needed. As they become teenagers, their needs change. They still need you, but in a different way. One of their greatest needs is to be seen, heard and understood by you.

EPILOGUE

That only comes through effective communication. As you build these communication bonds with your daughter, remember that her needs have changed, but she still loves you just as much as she did when she was little.

My prayer for you is that you will create wonderful memories of great conversations that you and your daughter have throughout the years. Not necessarily easy ones, but great ones. Ones where you showed up as your authentic self and ones where she felt trust, love and support. In the end, applying what is learned in this book has the power to change how women view themselves as they become adults and how they interact in many different types of relationships. This is powerful and important, mothers.

I hope your life has been changed in some way by this book. The last letter I'm going to share is extremely personal. It comes from my daughter, and I just want to show you that I too have issues with effective communication. Although I've remedied a lot of them, I still have room for growth. We all do. Will you continue to grow with me?

Dear Mom,

I think the first time that I can remember feeling like something was wrong was when my diary was read around age 10 or 11. It was a horrible, invasive feeling. I loved that little book so much. I remember taking it everywhere. After having another set of eyes on it, writing in it did not feel the same at all, and I definitely stopped carrying it around. If I had to guess, I'd say that was when I started to think about how our communication looked. I was punished for several things I wrote, so to me communication was a trap. I always knew, however, that if I was truly in a life or death situation, that I could come to you. But it was very difficult to feel understood, when it wasn't a dire emergency, and to this day I think I harbor some of those same feelings.

Growing into adulthood and gaining confidence has alleviated some of the fear of talking to you about sensitive things. There's still a level of judgment that I believe kind of quiets me. I take responsibility for that, but I can express myself in a way that at least I feel comfortable with. Overall, I don't know if I think our communication is great, but it's definitely better. I think healthy time and space separation really helps me to feel as if our relationship isn't forced or to "parentish" and allows me to enjoy the talking that does take place. I believe it could only get better.

Love always,
Tiara, 31

EPILOGUE

QUESTION

What are the 3 biggest takeaways that you have learned from this book?

ACTION

Celebrate yourself and your daughter in the way you like to celebrate best: ice cream date, photo shoot, movies. Just do it! You both are worth celebrating.

AFFIRMATION

I am worthy of celebration. I am strong, smart, bold and brave.

MEET THE AUTHOR

MOMMY ~ TEACHER ~ MENTOR

Miriam Arvinger is the mother of two adult children. She believes this is her greatest calling in this life - to raise well-rounded, compassionate, mentally and physically healthy, responsible human beings that share their respective gifts with their community and society. Her daughter and the many girls she's worked with over the years serve as the impetus for this book.

She is also a veteran educator who has been impacting the lives of youth and young adults for over 30 years. Miriam specializes in student motivation, youth development, professional development and training, and curriculum and program development. She is a passionate, fearless leader who innovates and executes lessons that adapt to students' needs inside and outside of the classroom.

One of Miriam's superpowers is connecting with youth and motivating them so that common goals can be achieved through coaching and mentorship. She has mentored thousands of girls and young women through a variety of programs and organizations, such as the Boys and Girls Clubs and Unidos, to name a few. She loves cultivating self-awareness, self-love and healthy self-esteem in young girls and women, so they can confidently cope with life's challenges.

Because Miriam recognizes the importance of education and mentorship, she desires to start a school that will train students in life skills and non-traditional courses, such as: financial literacy, puberty, self-identity and worth and entrepreneurship. It's coming!

Miriam is a graduate of Howard University (BA) and Liberty University (MA). This is her first of many books that will motivate, uplift and inspire others to be their very best.

APPENDIX

Resources For Further Help

Suggested Reading List

These books provide invaluable insight and wisdom on communication, healing and understanding ourselves and our daughters.

1. *The Gifts of Imperfection by Brene Brown* - a must read for moms struggling with perfectionism, vulnerability and shame. This book literally changed my life for the better because I was able to pinpoint my shame and expose it so it no longer controlled me.

2. *Nonviolent Communication: Create Your Life, Your Relationships, and Your World in Harmony with Your Values by Marshall B. Rosenberg* - provides much needed strategies for effective communication and helps the reader to understand

empathy, compassion, collaboration, courage and authenticity.

3. *Boundaries by Dr. Henry Cloud and Dr. John Townsend* - learn how to establish clear boundaries in all areas of your life. This is particularly helpful for those who have parents or family members that do not respect your boundaries, especially as it relates to raising your children. It will also give suggestions on how to establish boundaries with your daughter.

4. *The Birth Order Book by Dr. Kevin Leman* - gives great insight on why we do what we do and how our actions and behaviors are aligned with our birth order. It explains how birth order affects what you do and how you behave.

5. *Dear Sonali By Lynn Toler* - great words of wisdom from Judge Lynn Toler on what she would tell her daughter if she had one. Amazing insight and great advice.

6. *The Care and Keeping of You 1: The Body Book for Younger Girls by Valorie Schaefer* - priceless information, tips and facts on growing up, for girls 8 and up. You'll find answers to questions about your changing body, and everything from hair care to healthy eating, bad breath to bras and periods to pimples. This is a great refresher for mothers and daughters.

7. *The Care and Keeping of You 2: The Body Book for Older Girls by Dr. Cara Natterson* - provides great advice about growing up. This book covers new questions about periods, your growing body, peer pressure, personal care, and more! Written for

girls 10 and up and taps into some of the emotional changes girls go through.

FREE OR ALMOST FREE THERAPY RESOURCES:

Check out these sites for low-cost therapy. Also, most companies now offer free therapy services and resources for employees.

www.etherapypro.com
www.betterhelp.com
www.therapyforblackgirls.com
www.thelovelandfoundation.org
https://www.sondermind.com/blog

DETERMINE YOUR CORE VALUES

Core Values are strongly held beliefs that are important to you because they act as a set of rules and guidelines for events you encounter in life. Although you may not be fully aware of all your core values, you have them. There is a code of life that you live by based on what's important to you and what you value. Take one, or all, of the quizzes to find out your core values.

Some of the quizzes are quite long, so take them when you are relaxed and have time.

https://consciousendeavors.org/core-values-index/
https://dfdx.us/core-values-quiz/
https://personalvalu.es/

MINDSET QUIZ

Do you have a fixed or growth mindset? Take a quiz to find out.

https://tinyurl.com/2p9eycpm
https://wdhb.com/blog/growth-mindset-quiz/